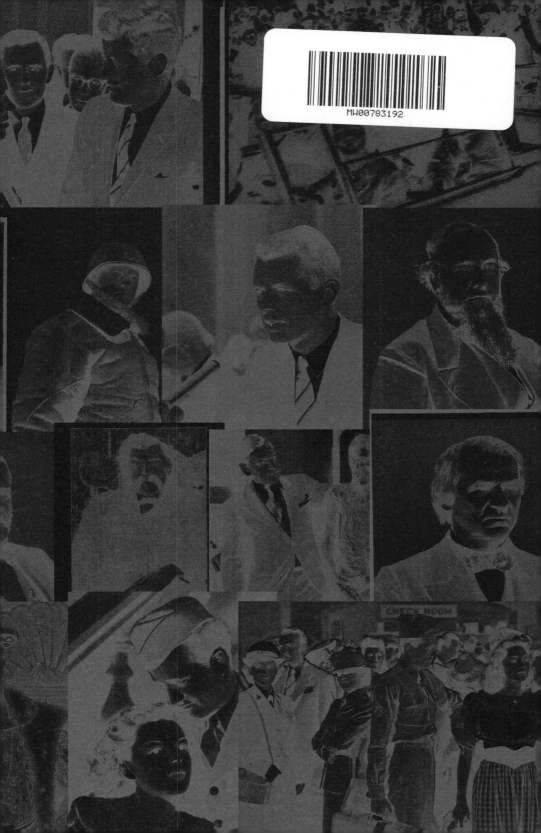

SPIRITS SPEAK

OF CONSPIRACIES

AND MYSTERIES

BARRY STROHM

4880 Lower Valley Road • Atglen, PA 19310

Copyright © 2017 by Barry Strohm

Library of Congress Control Number: 2016955385

Designed by RoS
Cover design by Matt Goodman

Type set in Courier New/New Century Schoolbook
ISBN: 978-0-7643-5269-0
Printed in China

Published by Schiffer Publishing, Ltd.
4880 Lower Valley Road
Atglen, PA 19310
Phone: (610) 593-1777; Fax: (610) 593-2002
E-mail: Info@schifferbooks.com
Web: www.schifferbooks.com

For our complete selection of fine books on this and related subjects, please visit our website at www.schifferbooks.com. You may also write for a free catalog.

Schiffer Publishing's titles are available at special discounts for bulk purchases for sales promotions or premiums. Special editions, including personalized covers, corporate imprints, and excerpts, can be created in large quantities for special needs. For more information, contact the publisher.

We are always looking for people to write books on new and related subjects. If you have an idea for a book, please contact us at proposals@schifferbooks.com.

AS I FINISHED THIS BOOK, I REALIZED THAT IT CAN ONLY BE DEDICATED TO A SINGLE PERSON: MY WIFE, CONNIE.

She has been my soul mate and wife for over fifty years. An incredible mother for my children, a role model for all and an inspiration for myself, she is truly one of a kind. Our journey through life has been long and sometimes arduous, but I have always known that I could not have done it without her. We are now in the final, incredible chapter of our lives, truly blessed by God.

CONSPIRACY THEORISTS OF THE WORLD—BELIEVERS IN THE HIDDEN HANDS OF THE ROTHSCHILDS AND THE MASONS AND THE ILLUMINATI—WE SKEPTICS OWE YOU AN APOLOGY. YOU WERE RIGHT. THE PLAYERS MAY BE A LITTLE DIFFERENT, BUT YOUR BASIC PREMISE IS CORRECT: THE WORLD IS A RIGGED GAME.

—MATT TAIBBI
ROLLING STONE **MAGAZINE**

CONTENTS

Webster defines a conspiracy as:

a secret plan made by two or more people to do something that is harmful or illegal, or the act of secretly planning to do something that is harmful or illegal.

Throughout history, evil individuals have planned events that have definitely harmed others. Sometimes the conspiracies are so insidious that the general population does not even realize they have been harmed. Free choice and ego have a lot to do with the events shaping history that are recounted in this book.

I use our gift of spirit communication to contact the spirits of the actual individuals involved with some of the most famous conspiracies and mysteries throughout history. Whenever a spirit comes through during a session, we make a point to ask detailed historical questions to prove we have the presence of the actual spirit and not an imposter. In instances where we cannot contact the actual spirit involved with the incident, we ask the master guides to provide the required information. The historical detail that is provided by the guides and the souls of the spirits involved will amaze you.

At times, the information involved the deaths or harm of famous individuals. In some instances, such as the killing of Billy the Kid, you will see that the conspiracy involved an attempt to cover up a serious mistake, such as Pat Garrett shooting an innocent person in the back. You will see that Butch Cassidy outsmarted law enforcement and lived a long life, contrary to the ending you saw in the famous movie. We have even asked the spirit guides what happened to notorious teamster president Jimmy Hoffa.

I discuss historical and contemporary conspiracies that are currently affecting our daily lives such as government manipulation of the weather and chemtrails. In one chapter I delve into the greatest aeronautical mystery of all time: the disappearance of Malaysian Filght 370 and why the wreckage will in all probability never be found. As you will see, conspiracies have changed the path of history and are affecting the future of all of us.

From King Richard III to John F. Kennedy the souls on the other side of the life veil are anxious for the truths concerning their demise to be known. President Kennedy went into great detail about the infamous day in Dallas when he was assassinated. His spirit told the truth about whether Oswald pulled the trigger or not and who really gave the orders to carry out the killing of an American president.

Not only does this book tell who was behind the killing of Abraham Lincoln, it relates the facts that show John Wilkes Booth was not killed by soldiers but lived until 1903. Included is a picture from the Library of Congress that shows the body of Booth in a coffin taken in Enid, Oklahoma, during 1903 and his mummified remains. When you see the picture of the individual in the casket you will be amazed at the resemblance to earlier pictures of Booth.

Conspiracies of the past are not only confined to political figures. One chapter deals with the life of Robert Walker, a well-known actor from the 1940s. We delve into who knew what when the Twin Towers were attacked and if weapons of mass destruction really existed at the beginning of the Gulf War. In the final chapter of the book we also examine the process by which the books of the New Testament of the Bible were selected and the omission of vital gospels. We even discuss the Ark of the Covenant and the Holy Grail.

Some of the greatest conspiracies are created by our governments. In this book you will learn that our weather has been influenced by manipulation of the ionosphere through the HAARP program and the seeding of clouds for many years. You will also learn of the potential for rogue countries to manipulate the weather as a weapon of war. We investigate chemtrails and the purpose behind them, a subject that is of interest to any of us who breathe the air around us. In perhaps the worst of the historical tragedies you will find out the true fate of one of our greatest military heroes, General George Patton.

In my previous book, *Aliens Among Us: Exploring Past and Present*, I indicated that aliens are not only a reality but have visited Earth since the time of the dinosaurs. You will learn the real reason why the major governments have gone to such lengths to keep the truth from the public and how long the conspiracy of secrecy has been taking place. The role of extraterrestrials in the development of the atomic bomb during World War II as well as the amazing progress of the German rocket program during that time period are examined in detail.

The tool we use to communicate with the spirits is known as a talking or question board. Talking boards have been used in one form or another for thousands of years. Not to be confused with a Ouija board, ours has actually been designed by the spirits during channeling sessions. The guides themselves gave us the shape and configuration of the board. In addition, they want it to be called "the question board." All our sessions are recorded in video and audio and the record of every word of the souls interviewed is stored in files in my computer.

In addition, the spirit guides have even given us a prayer of protection that we repeat at the beginning of every session. Here are the exact words of prayer given us by the guides:

GOD PLEASE GRANT US YOUR WISDOM AND PROTECTION. GRANT US THE KNOWLEDGE THAT WE CAN HANDLE AND KEEP US SAFE FROM ALL THINGS THAT WILL HARM US. KEEP THE MESSAGES POSITIVE AND PURE LOVE. KEEP US SAFE FROM OUR OWN EGO. WE ASK THESE THINGS IN THE LIGHT OF THE SEEN, THE UNSEEN, AND THE HONESTY OF GOD.

The board has a glass cover and we use a slider constructed out of quartz that resembles a shot glass. Quartz is a crystal that helps increase the energy of the spirits attempting to give us a message and makes it easier to get their message through accurately. The glass surface is lubricated with an oil to help the pointer slide easily to the letters or numbers. Two of us put our fingers on the quartz glass slider and, when we ask questions, the spirit guides move the glass to the letters and the letters spell out the message. A third person writes the letters down so we can keep track of the messages as they are given to us. Every word of the spirits quoted in this book was received on a question board such as the one shown. This type of spirit communication allows us to receive the messages accurately and in detail.

By this stage, I am sure many of you are skeptical of our ability to gain information from spirits on the other side of the life veil and especially our ability to gain information from the likes of Jack Kennedy or General Patton. You can rest assured that the spirits want their stories told accurately, not what has often been written in the history books. I have attempted to tell their stories as accurately as possible from the session transcripts. Throughout the book, the words of the spirits are printed in blue. Please approach this book with an open mind and feel free to research the included statements. Keep in mind that I am only repeating the words of the spirits, so please don't shoot the messenger. It is my belief that you will never look at our written history in the same manner again.

The question board, the channeling device designed by the spirit guides.
Courtesy Barry Strohm.

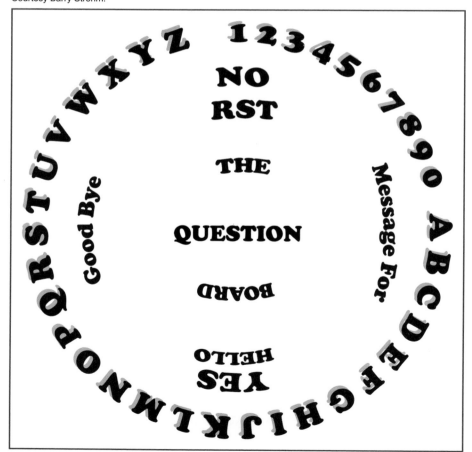

ACKNOWLEDGMENTS

All of the events and information in this book were obtained through the use of a special channeling board that, in contrast to a Ouija board, uses a glass-on-glass surface. The original design of the board dates back over forty years when Sam and Carol Green of Salt Lake City, Utah, pioneered its design. We were taught to use the board by Carol's daughter, K, and her husband, Doc Kivett. Much of the channeling information was gained in sessions where the two of them would be on the board and I would ask the questions. At times we would conduct the interviews over Skype with them being in Salt Lake while we were in Pennsylvania. Without their help this book could never have been written. Carol's other daughter, Sammi Tall, is also working with us in channeling sessions and has contributed greatly.

Any of you who have read my previous books, *Afterlife, What Really Happens on the Other Side,* and *Aliens Among Us: Past and Present*, know that we had the privilege of working with the clairvoyant Barbara Lee Rowe. You will see that several of the chapters are based on information gained in sessions where she was present. Her contributions to this volume are numerous and highly appreciated.

We have been conducting our current channeling sessions with Marian Beattie, a very gifted medium. She has proven invaluable in helping contact many of the spirits telling their stories in this book. Marian brings another dimension to our ability to communicate with the spirits on the other side of the life veil.

Throughout this book you will hear me refer to our spirit guides. We have been blessed with the ability to contact these guides that provide information and assist in bringing forward human spirits that have their stories to tell. I would like to give a special thanks to our guides, Raz, Mou, Sterling, and many others that have provided the information recorded herein.

THE KILLING OF GENERAL GEORGE PATTON

What you are about to read is one of the most unbelievable conspiracies contained in this book. When the information was first given to me in our channeling session with General Patton, I thought it was inconceivable that the events you are about to read could take place at the command of our political and military leaders. During three different channeling sessions I challenged the General to give me information that would conclusively prove that we were indeed communicating with the proper spirit. As you will see, he gave information in support of his story that I feel is above reproach. I am about to relay the details of a great American tragedy in the exact words of the spirit of General George S. Patton Jr.

GREAT AMERICAN HERO

One of our greatest military heroes, General George S. Patton Jr. was a brilliant and very complex individual. Born to a well-to-do military family, whose exploits dated to the Revolutionary War, on November 11, 1881, there was never any doubt that he would serve his country. He attended Virginia Military Institute and then went on to graduate from West Point in 1909, commissioned a second lieutenant in the 15th Cavalry Regiment. A superb athlete, he competed in 1912 Stockholm Olympics representing the United States in the first Modern Pentathlon.

His first combat came when he was assigned to General John J. Pershing's expedition into Mexico against Francisco "Pancho" Vila. With the advent of World War I, he was assigned to and took command of the United States Tank Corps. By 1917, he had participated in the World's first tank battle at Cambrai, France. The victorious Patton was wounded in the leg and received the Distinguished Service Cross.

His experiences in WWI convinced him that armored warfare was the way of the future. Congress proved unwilling to allocate funds for such a command, but he continued to develop improved communication systems and weapons for the tanks remaining in the Army. By 1932, he had graduated from the Army War College in Carlisle, Pennsylvania. The success of the German Blitzkrieg during the late 1930s finally convinced Congress that the United States needed a strong armored unit, and, in 1940, our leaders finally created the Armored Divisions. By April 11, 1941, Patton was named commanding general of the Second Armored Division at Ft. Benning, Georgia.

WORLD WAR II

On December 7, 1941, Japan attacked Pearl Harbor and the United States was faced with another World War. German Panzer Divisions overran Europe and Northern Africa. Nazi forces in Africa were under the command of Field Marshal Erwin Rommel, a brilliant and experienced armored commander. General Patton's first test against the German war machine would be leading the all-American

General George S. Patton.
Courtesy US Archives.

task force in Operation Torch, the Allied invasion of North Africa. After executing a series of brilliant maneuvers, Rommel was defeated, and Patton assumed command of the 7th Army in Sicily, the next phase of the Allied advance. His great military achievements during the Sicily campaign increased his fame in the United States but inflamed the ire of General Bernard Montgomery, head of British operations in Sicily and soon to become the field marshal of English operations in Europe. The outspoken General's enemies got their chance when he inspected a field hospital during the Sicily fighting.

In early August 1943, the General's disregard for the concept of battle fatigue led to a major incident that almost ended his military career. On August 3 and 10, he slapped and berated two soldiers under his command, who were in the hospital with no obvious wounds other than battle fatigue. General Eisenhower and Chief of Staff George C. Marshall made the decision not to fire him but make him apologize to his men and then removed their best fighting commander from active participation in the war.

Eisenhower, instead, put him in charge of Operation Fortitude where the general acted as a decoy to fool Hitler into thinking that the invasion would take place at positions other than the beaches of Normandy. Hitler firmly believed the European invasion would take place near the town of Calais, France, under the command of General Patton. When the Normandy invasion took place, Hitler held Panzer Divisions in place, still thinking that Normandy was a secondary attack and that the main invasion would take place under the Allies best fighting commander. Patton actually had a huge impact on the success of Operation Overlord, without participating personally.

COMMAND OF THE 3RD ARMY

After the Normandy invasion, Patton was placed as commander of the 3rd Army and participated in repelling the Nazi advances at the Battle of the Bulge and spearheaded successfully the attack on Germany. His exploits rescuing the 101st Airborne Division at Bastogne is regarded as one of the monumental achievement in military history. As the war entered the closing days, General Patton became more aware of the menace that the Soviet Union presented to the postwar western nations. He began to publicly call for continuing the War and fighting the Soviets while they could be defeated. The war hero was planning to go back to the United States to argue his case. Since America was very pro-Soviet at this time, neither our Government nor the Soviets wanted the brash general to make the argument to the American people.

The wartime president, Franklin Delano Roosevelt, had died on April 12, 1945, leaving Harry S. Truman as president and commander in chief to conclude the War. One of Roosevelt's great projects was to create the United Nations after the fighting ended. In order to have the Soviet Union cooperate, they were essentially promised all of Eastern Europe and a large part of Berlin. Truman, the new commander in chief, was committed to following along the path created by Roosevelt. The direct-speaking General Patton represented a problem for both the United States and the Soviet Union.

After VE day, the general returned to the United States where he was greeted with huge parades and crowds. His immense popularity drew the attention of other generals and politicians. The outspoken Patton could be a major problem for the Washington establishment. With the war still going on in the Pacific, Patton hoped for a command in the anticipated invasion of Japan. General Douglas MacArthur turned down the application of the famed hero of the European campaign to participate in the planning for and execution of the Pacific theatre invasion of the Japanese mainland. In retrospect, it appears MacArthur did not want to share the spotlight of the American people.

The Third Army was responsible for administering the reconstruction of Bavaria, and General Patton returned to oversee the rebuilding of the war-torn country. For the time being, he was pretty much out of the public eye as the war in the Pacific came an abrupt end with the use of the atomic bomb.

IN THE HEADLINES, AGAIN

On September 22, the general held a news conference that would catapult him back to the scrutiny of his commanding officers and the politicians. As part of the Bavarian rebuilding process, Patton had retained the services of individuals who had served in the Nazi party, since they had the experience to fill some of the vacant positions. A reporter asked the outspoken general why he retained former Nazis in his office. Here is his exact answer to the question:

I despise and abhor Nazis and Hitlerism as much as anyone. My record on that is clear and unchallengeable. It is to be found on battlefields from Morocco to Bad Tolz. In supervising the functioning of the Bavarian government, which is my mission, the first thing that happened was that the outs accused the ins of being Nazis. Now, more than half the German people were Nazis and we would be in a hell of a fix if we removed all Nazi party members from office.

The way I see it, this Nazi question is very much like a Democratic and Republican election fight. To get things done in Bavaria, after the virtually complete disorganization and disruption of four years of war, we had to compromise with the devil a little. We had no alternative but to turn to people who knew what to do and how to do it, So, for the time being we are compromising with the devil to that extent.

It's regrettable, but a very urgent and vital job has to be done to put this shattered country back on its feet again. We are trying to do that as best we can with the personnel available. That's the whole story.

I don't like Nazis any more than you do. I despise them. In the past three years I did my utmost to kill as many of them as possible. Now we are using them for lack of anyone better until we can get better people."
(www.pattonhq.com/textfiles/resign.html)

His answer made perfect sense except for one little thing; he seemed to compare Democrats and Republicans to Nazis. Much like today, his comments were taken out of context and his detractors on the radio and newspapers blew his statement out of proportion. The next day he offered a statement of apology in which he referred to the comparison as an "unfortunate analogy."

TOO MANY ENEMIES

General Eisenhower jumped on the opportunity to deride the outspoken Patton and deemed the apology as insufficient. He was ordered to attend a face-to-face with Eisenhower that lasted two-and-one-half hours in which he was ordered to dismiss any Nazis serving in the Bavarian government. By October 5, he was relieved of command of the 3rd Army and reassigned to the 15th Army, basically an administrative unit and military on paper only. General George Patton, the hero of the Battle of the Bulge, was furious over his demotion.

When a general officer retires from the Army, he is still obligated to honor a code of conduct that precludes them from speaking negatively about their former commanding officers, including the president, the supreme commander. Apparently Patton devised a plan where he was going to quit outright, not retire. He was independently wealthy and did not have to worry about an Army pension. This would allow him to speak his mind in public and he had a lot to say. He confided his plans with his chief of staff, General Gay. When he told

General Gay the following, it probably sent events in motion that would result in his demise:

> *When I get home, I am going through with my plan to resign from the Army. I'm going to do it with a statement that will be remembered a long time. If it doesn't make big headlines, I'll be surprised. As I told you, I am determined to be free to live my own way of life, and I'm going to make that unforgettably clear.* (www.pattonhq.com/textfiles/resign.html)

On the pretext of getting General Patton to relax, General Gay made arrangements for the two of them to go on a hunting trip. On the morning of December 9, 1945, the two of them set off in Patton's command car, a 1938 Cadillac, Model 75. According to military reports, his trusted driver, PFC Horace Woodring, was driving the vehicle near the city of Mannheim, Germany. There was a light mist on that morning. What follows is what the Army says happened.

THE OFFICIAL VERSION OF THE ACCIDENT

According to the official Army reports, while driving at approximately 35 miles an hour, a two-and-one-half-ton 6×6 GMC truck driven by twenty-year-old T/5 Robert L. Thompson from Camden, New Jersey, made a sudden turn in front of the command vehicle with no hand signal. Woodring had no chance to avoid a collision and ran into the truck crushing the right front fender of the Cadillac. In

spite of the relatively minor nature of the accident, General Patton was thrown forward and struck his head on a metal railing that was above the drivers' seat, breaking his neck and causing a laceration to his head. The story is that Patton fell across the lap of General Gay, paralyzed and bleeding. Neither Gay nor Woodring sustained any injury. Coincidentally, the first vehicle to appear was an ambulance with a medic, Sargent Leroy Ogden, inside. The general was loaded into the ambulance and taken to the 130th Station Hospital of the Seventh Army where he was supposedly admitted approximately one hour after the accident.

He was treated for the dislocation/fracture of his neck and placed in a cast. His condition improved rapidly, and the authorities were actually considering shipping him back to the United States. According to reports, his condition suddenly took a turn for the worse due to a lack of oxygen in the blood and a pulmonary embolism. It is said he died in his sleep on December 21, 1945, with his wife at his side. He was buried at the US Military Cemetery at Hamm, Luxembourg, the highest-ranking US officer to ever be buried on foreign soil.

As I did the research for this book I ran across several articles that implied that the death of Patton was not an accident and that it had perhaps been planned by the Soviets. Russia was about to take over Eastern Europe without firing a shot, so the last thing they wanted was a beloved military hero preaching that the US should defeat them while they had a chance. Patton had also made many enemies among US Generals and politicians. After all, he had compared them to Nazis. I decided to attempt to reach the spirit of the General and ask him what had happened during the accident. I was in no way prepared for some of his answers.

American WWII grave sites in Germany.
Courtesy Dollarphotoclub.

The first time we reached the spirit of General Patton was in July 2015 in Park City, Utah. Sammi Tall and I were on the channeling board as I asked for the spirit of the general. When I asked if the spirit of the general was currently with us, the answer was:

YES.

Whenever we are blessed with the presence of a great historical figure, I am always a bit overwhelmed. I stated that we were honored to have him with us, that he had an incredible war record and was a great general. He replied:

YES, I WAS.

No one ever accused George Patton of modesty. I always try to verify that we are really communicating with the actual spirit, so I began with historical questions looking for specific facts. First I asked where he was born.

SAN GABRIEL.

That was indeed where General Patton was born in 1885. Next I asked how old he was when he passed.

78

Not even close! According to all reports, he was killed in an accident in Germany at the age of sixty from a broken neck incurred when his command vehicle collided with a truck. I pursued the discrepancy by inquiring his cause of death.

OLD AGE.

That answer differed greatly from the official cause of death, namely lack of oxygen in the blood and a pulmonary embolism resulting from his accident. I was beginning to wonder if we had the wrong spirit and he was playing with us. Trying to understand what I was hearing, my follow up was: Are you telling me you were not killed in the accident in Germany?

NO.

I reworded the question so there would be no misunderstanding: You are telling me that you survived the accident in Germany.

YES.

I was expecting to try to find out if the Russians were responsible for his murder. The interview was not starting out like anything I expected. After trying to think up some responsible question, I asked him what city he was in when he passed. His answer did nothing to help solve the mystery of what he was disclosing.

San Francisco.

Instead of dying of a broken neck in Germany at the age of sixty, he passed of old age at seventy-eight in San Francisco! The official reports made a big deal that he was buried with his fallen comrades in Germany. When I inquired where he was buried, the reply was:

At sea.

This was shaping up as a conspiracy beyond my wildest expectations. Are you saying the casket in Germany does not hold your body?

Yes.

I thought I would back up a bit and verify some basic information. I asked if there was an accident in 1945.

Yes.

Did they attempt to murder you?

Yes.

Were the Russians involved?

No.

Since the Soviets had nothing to do with the accident, I inquired if he was saying that our own military was behind what happened to him.

Yes.

As the interview progressed, I was having a lot of trouble getting a grip on what I was being told. I had always held General Eisenhower in high regard. I asked if General Eisenhower was aware of the events that took place.

Yes.

I could not imagine that General Eisenhower would have plotted to kill one of our most famous commanders, even if there was no love lost between them. My next question was who gave the order to carry out the operation. His answer was not too surprising.

The Pres.

Franklin Roosevelt died in April 1945, so Harry Truman would have been president of the United States. When I asked the spirit of the general what he thought of Truman, his answer was:

He was a snake.

The general was never one to not say what was on his mind. Did Truman know about your captivity?

President Harry Truman.
Courtesy US Archives.

YES, BIG PLOT.

A big plot had to have someone behind it. My next question inquired who was responsible for the plan.

EISENHOWER.

I was still having a lot of trouble understanding why our own military would attempt to assassinate one of our best-fighting generals. My next question addressed what provoked our own military to carry out such a plan. His answer was short and to the point.

BECAUSE OF WHAT I KNEW.

Will you tell me what you knew that caused this?

NO.

I knew from other interviews with military spirits that they guard their secrets closely. General Patton was no exception. Old ways die hard. I tried again to find out the motive for what had happened by asking for examples of what type of collusion he knew they were going to carry out.

MORE MURDERS.

General Eisenhower gave specific orders for the 3rd Army not to take Berlin even though there would have been little resistance from the Germans. I asked: Why were you stopped from going into Berlin before the Soviets got there?

TO STOP THE PEOPLE THEY WERE ROUNDING UP TO KILL. I WAS GOING TO STOP THEM.

Deciding it was time to get some more details about the accident, I asked him how he got his neck broken in the accident in Germany. As you recall the official report was that he hit his head on a metal handle in the car.

I WAS HUNG.

No way was I ready for that answer. After catching my breath my next question was: How were you hung?

THEY HUNG ME FIRST.

Can you describe what happened when they tried to hang you?

THERE WAS A STRUGGLE. THEN I WAS DRUGGED.

Were you alive after they tried to hang you? I think that was a redundant question.

YES.

Why would they try to hang you?

IF FOUND IT WOULD GIVE DENIABILITY.

Are you trying to say they wanted to make it look like the Nazi holdouts captured you and tried to hang you?

YES.

Your vehicle was supposedly driven by your trusted driver; was he involved?"

NO, KILLED HIM.

How long after the accident was he killed?

DRUGGED.

Do you know the name of the man that was responsible for the attempted hanging?

YES.

With a lead-in like that I had to ask for the name of the person that gave the order to carry out such a plan. He replied:

TRUMAN.

You are referring to President Truman?

YES.

You said you died in San Francisco. Are you saying you were kidnapped and held prisoner?

KIND OF.

I was having a real hard time understanding what he was saying. Are you saying you were held prisoner in a military hospital until you died?

YES.

Were you an invalid?

YES.

Were you in a coma?

NO.

Could you speak?

YES.

Did you ever attempt to tell anyone you were being held prisoner?

No.

What name were you called during your time in the hospital?

Doc.

Why didn't you try to tell someone who you were and that you were being held against your will?

They would have killed me.

Did they do anything to alter your appearance?

I became weak and thin.

When I began the interview I had prepared a lot of questions concerning the different aspects of his accident as the facts according to official information were released through the years. The statements I was receiving on the channeling board were contrary to anything I had ever heard or were even hinted at. What I needed was some time to digest what had just been told to me, but I knew there were going to be a lot more questions to be answered. I asked the general if there was any more information that he would like to give us at this time. He replied:

You will get more information later.

Are you saying you will come back again for us?

Yes.

On that note, Sammi and I ended our first session with General Patton. Many questions were whirling through my head concerning what we had just heard. There was no doubt in my mind that we had a lot more to talk about. Our next opportunity to gain more information came several weeks later after my wife, Connie, and I traveled back to New Oxford, Pennsylvania. The next time we tried to contact General Patton, Marian Beattie and I were doing the board channeling. Marian is a clairvoyant and can often visualize in her mind the individual being interviewed, and I was looking forward to bringing her abilities to the session. This session took place the end of July, 2015.

THE SECOND INTERVIEW

The spirit of the famous general was ready and able to communicate with us. I started the session off by asking for information that would confirm that we were really in his presence. My first question inquired as to his age at passing. This was an identical question I asked during the last session. He answered:

78.

Same as last session! Next, I asked what year he passed.

1963.

I thought I would test him with a trick question. I said: That means you were a prisoner for sixteen years.

No, 18.

He was as sharp as ever. No way was he going to get trapped with bad math. According to the information he had given, eighteen years was the correct answer, an unbelievable time to be held prisoner in an invalid body. He mentioned that he was held in San Francisco at a military hospital. My next question would also test the validity of his comments. I asked the address of the hospital in San Francisco.

AT VA NOBS HILLSIDE.

The San Francisco VA hospital is near Nobs Hill. My next question was how long was he held at the San Francisco hospital. He answered:

12.

In our earlier interview he had mentioned being held for eighteen years. When I asked if he was held at more than one facility he replied:

YES, VA.

Are you telling me you were held at another hospital in Virginia?

YES, 6 YEARS.

I figured if he could give me the address of the hospital in Virginia it would offer conclusive proof that I was indeed talking to General Patton. When I asked if he knew the address of the hospital, once again his answer was not what I expected.

NO, IT WAS UNDERGROUND.

So you are saying that after being held the first six years at an underground VA hospital in Virginia, you were moved to San Francisco.

YES.

I really hadn't considered that we would have underground hospital sites, so I decided to do a little research into underground facilities maintained by our government. Apparently, since the beginning of the cold war in the 1950s, they have constructed a multitude of bases located deep underground. For additional research on this subject, I would recommend checking out www. subterraneanbases.com. If this website is anywhere near correct, we would have the ability to hide anyone for many years in a secret facility.

A PROBLEM WITH THE GENERAL'S
STORY

One of the major discrepancies from the first session was when he told me that they had drugged and killed his driver. When I did some research, I learned that the person the army attributed to driving the car at the time of the accident, PFC Horace Woodring, died at the age of seventy-seven in 2003. When I asked him to explain the discrepancy he replied:

DIFFERENT MAN.

What was the name of your driver at the time of the accident?

I CALLED HIM SCRAGG.

Did you trust Scragg to drive you around?

YES.

None of the official reports ever mentioned a driver other than PFC Woodring. I asked if they killed Scragg to keep him quiet.

YES, DRUGGED.

It was becoming very apparent that this was a very well-planned operation and anyone that got in the way was eliminated. My next question was if they forced PFC Woodring to say, on fear of death, that he was at the wheel of the car at the time of the accident. He replied:

YES.

General Gay was Patton's chief of staff at the time of the accident. The accounts of the accident say that it was General Gay who proposed they go pheasant hunting. When I asked if his chief of staff was involved, he answered:

YES, UNDER ORDERS.

Did General Gay set you up by asking you to go pheasant hunting?

HIS SECOND ASKED.

Do you remember his name?

MILLNER.

Did General Gay participate in the attempt to hang you?

YES, BUT HE WAS PERIPHERAL.

I had read an account of the accident that stated General Paul Harkin was present. When I asked the question of General Patton, he answered:

NO.

The newspaper reports at the time of the accident made a big deal about Patton's wife visiting the General while he was in the hospital in Germany. One report I read mentioned that she would read to him during the night and she was with him when he passed. I asked if his wife had ever visited while he was in Germany.

NO.

So much for the newspaper articles. I restated the question so there would be no misunderstanding: So the newspaper report of your wife being at you bedside in Germany was a lie?

YES.

There seemed to be a lot of discrepancies involving the stories about his wife and how she responded when he was in the hospital in Germany. I asked if at the time of the accident they convinced his wife that he was dead.

YES.

Did your wife ever find out you were still alive?

LATER ON.

How did your wife find out you were alive?

SHE WAS BROUGHT TO ME BY PRIVATE MONTGOMERY, MY GUARD AND NURSE. IT WAS A KINDNESS.

Are you saying that he snuck her into the hospital?

YES.

It was only through the kindness of his nurse and guard that in those long eighteen years he ever got to see his wife again and that was because he broke the rules and sneaked her into the facility. When I asked how many times in total he got to see her the answer was:

3. I DID NOT WANT HER TO SEE ME DIMINISHED.

It seemed inconceivable that this could have been carried out in a high-security facility. I asked if the government ever found out about her visits.

YES.

I could not see how that could end well for the participants. My next question was: What happened?

SHE WAS NOT A THREAT TO THEM.

My guess is that when they found out about the visits, they moved him to

San Francisco. I asked him: You were in San Francisco for many years; did she ever visit you there?

No.

For a plan of this magnitude to be executed and carried out over eighteen years there had to be many high-ranking individuals involved. We had already discussed the involvement of President Truman, but I thought I would pursue others involved in the plot. William Donovan was the wartime chief of the Office of Strategic Services, predecessor to the CIA. This office was the WWII equivalent of the Central Intelligence Agency. When I asked if Donovan was involved in the plot his answer was:

Yes.

When I asked which general was directly responsible for the incident, he answered:

7.

One advantage to having a clairvoyant participate in a channeling session is they can often see and hear in their mind the participating spirit. At this point of the session, Marian broke in and said she could see an individual in military dress, and he kept saying the word "assholes." There was no doubt in my mind she was seeing General Patton say what he thought of those participating in the conspiracy. My next question pursued what assholes participated in the plan: So the plan came from the top down and involved the whole chain of command?

Yes.

That was a much milder reply than I expected! Since the general claims that Truman and Eisenhower were involved in the plan he could certainly anticipate there would be no mercy from them while they were serving as president. But if he did not pass until 1963, there were several years when Jack Kennedy was president. I inquired if Kennedy ever knew the General was being held against his will.

No.

I told the General that we had interviewed him in a previous session and that he impressed us as being a good man. When questioned if the general ever met Kennedy while on the other side, he replied:

Yes.

It must be really interesting when all the famous people get together on the other side. One can only imagine the conversations. I asked him what President Kennedy said to him when he found out what happened. The answer did not surprise me.

He wept for a future lost.

When I asked if he ever saw President Roosevelt on the other side, he stated:

YES.

Next, I asked if they got along over there and received a different answer.

NO, KARMA.

My guess is that there is a lot of animosity left over from when Roosevelt was involved in having the general removed from command. I knew from previous sessions that there are realms on the other side where souls are sent because of their decisions and behavior in the last incarnate lives. Being president of the United States does not assure a good spot in heaven. I asked if President Roosevelt was in a lower lever and the reply was:

YES.

General Patton was a very complex individual in life. As we discussed earlier, he was stripped of his command in Italy for slapping a soldier with battle fatigue. While slapping a soldier is certainly not on the approved list of things to do, removing the best field commander when we were in a time of war always seemed a bit harsh. I inquired if he had really slapped the soldier and he answered:

YES.

When I asked if that was the real reason he lost command of his army, he replied:

COMMANDER THOUGHT I KNEW TOO MUCH.

Were you set up when you lost your command?

YES.

Were you really anti-Semitic?

YES.

Was that part of the reason for your removal?

YES.

The General was answering all the hard questions truthfully!

FINDING JUSTICE

As we came to the end of our sessions with the general, I wanted to assure that he was pleased and that no critical information was missed during our interviews. When I inquired if there was any additional information he wanted included in this chapter, he gave me several messages. The first ending message was:

THERE WILL BE JUSTICE; I WILL SEE TO IT.

He had mentioned that his return was imminent, so I inquired if he was going to find justice after his return. He replied:

NO, BEFORE.

Spirits, especially such a strong personality as General Patton, can work miracles from the other side. Throughout our interviews, I was beginning to think there was more to my being introduced to the spirit than met the eye. When I asked if my book was part of his plan to seek justice, he said:

YES.

FAMILY TIES

My next question addressed how I'd decided to communicate with the spirit of the General. I really was not expecting his answer.

NO, SON, I FOUND YOU.

The fact that the great General George Patton sought me out to help him find justice was and is emotionally overwhelming. I must admit that after hearing that message, I was at a loss for words, and that does not often happen. On that note, I thanked the general and mentioned that we would need to speak again after I got my thoughts together.

As we were sitting around the channeling board, Marian mentioned that she was sensing there was a relationship between the general and myself. When Raz, our master guide, returned, I asked him if the general was part of my soul family. He answered in the negative.

NO.

When I asked why the general picked me for this mission, I think Raz paid me a compliment.

IN THIS WAY, YOUR LIGHT ATTRACTS MANY.

I am not sure Connie would totally agree with that. Next, I inquired if the general and I were related in any way.

YOU HAVE CROSSED PATHS.

In prior lives?

YES, 5 TIMES.

Needless to say, I was quite anxious to pursue that little tidbit of information.

A week later we were channeling for a third time and I asked the general to give me more details about how our souls had crossed paths in prior lives.

THERE WERE 2 FAMILY, ONE BROTHER AND ONE UNCLE.

What he meant is that I was a brother of General Patton's in one of his past lives! My next question inquired in what year we were brothers.

100 AD.

No wonder I did not remember! When I asked what country we lived in, he said:

PERSIA.

Souls really get around with this reincarnation thing. I was still having trouble understanding that he had picked me to help him find justice, even if we were distant relatives. When I asked him that question, he replied:

BECAUSE YOU CAN HEAR AND PASS IT ON.

REINCARNATION

Throughout his lifetime, General Patton believed that he had fought many battles in prior lives. If you watch the movie *Patton,* you will find a scene where he is in Africa and states that he fought at that spot with the Carthaginians. I asked him what wars he fought in prior lives.

MANY SMALL WARS. OURS IS A VIOLENT HISTORY. WARS TO PROTECT, TO CONQUER, FOR REVENGE. ALL MY LIVES HAD SOMETHING TO FIGHT FOR.

When I mentioned the scene from the movie and asked if he did indeed fight with the Carthaginians, he replied:

YES.

We were definitely talking to the soul of a true warrior! I inquired if he was happy over there.

OK. I AM READY TO COME BACK.

Are you coming back to be a leader in our government?

I HOPE SO, SOON.

It seemed as though he returned to fight in most of our major wars. The fact that he was getting ready to return brought up another question. I asked if he was coming back to fight in another major war. I did not take a lot of comfort in his answer.

We will see.

I wanted to know: Is there another major war in our future? The glass pointer never moved, he refused to answer. This was probably not a good sign for what will take place in the future.

OPINIONS OF GENERAL PATTON

What was your opinion of the movie, *Patton*?

It was right on in most places.

Did you approve of the way George Scott portrayed you?

Yes.

Have you met him on the other side?

Oh, yes.

Do you see General Rommel over there?

Yes, OK guy.

Do you get along with him?

Yes.

Do you see him often?"

No.

What do you think of Omar Bradley?

He had some good things to offer.

What do you think of Winston Churchill?

Asshole.

No question he was speaking his mind. I figured I would get a very strong answer concerning the next individual. I asked what he thought of Field Marshal Montgomery.

A man whose ego surpassed his intellect. Ha, Ha, Ha.

He thought it was funny that his answer was far from what I expected. As a change of pace I asked him what he thought of the Muslim extremists who are creating havoc in our modern world. This time his answer was what I expected.

Destructors. I'd have conquered them before they spread. Now the snake will spread, even if you cut off the head.

Maybe his coming back will have something to do with destroying the snake.

A VERY SPECIAL GREETING

Connie struck up a conversation with the general at one of our sessions. Her father, now ninety-four years of age, was assigned to the 3rd Army and fought under the command of General Patton in Europe. Holding three Purple Hearts and having been wounded in three different countries, her father speaks very highly of the general. On several occasions he told her how he was a good man as well as a very effective commander. She told the general of her father and how he felt about the general. When she finished speaking, we received the message:

I WILL GREET HIM.

As we finished the message, Marian commented that she could see the general standing and saluting. Not only was the general going to meet Connie's father when he passed to the other side, but he was showing his appreciation for a man that had served under him with distinction.

SUMMING IT ALL UP

As we came to the end of our channeling time together, I realized that one of his great regrets was that he did not have the opportunity to stop the Soviets from rounding up and executing many at the end of the war while his 3rd Army was ordered into inactivity. As I wrote the chapter, I could feel his spirit presence on many occasions. One day I took a break from writing his chapter to sit at my desk and eat a leisurely lunch. As I was sitting there and relaxing, I clearly heard the words in my head "can't you eat faster!" The general obviously had other places to go.

One evening I asked him if he had read my chapter about him and he replied:

YES.

When I asked if there was anything he wanted me to add his reply was:

PRESERVE THE DIGNITY OF THOSE THAT FELL TO AMERICA'S BETRAYAL.

That seems to be a message for the ages as our country once again fails to act as extremism in many forms is taking innocent lives, and we fail to learn the lessons of history and sit idly by. At the end of our sessions, I asked if there was a final message that he would like for me to put in the book. In my opinion, this statement summed up the will and character of this great man.

I DIED A PRISONER, BUT I WAS NEVER BROKEN. ∞

CHAPTER 2

LINCOLN AND BOOTH

CONSPIRACY

While investigating the murder of Abraham Lincoln, I became aware that there was not only a conspiracy surrounding the assassination of the president, but also of what really happened to the person who fired the fatal shot, John Wilkes Booth. During an earlier special session with Ulysses Grant, we were told who was behind the plan as well as some background surrounding the event in Ford's Theatre. In subsequent channeling sessions, I asked the spirit guides what really happened. As you read this chapter, I think some of the information that was confirmed by the guides will change how you look at the official history surrounding the event.

THE WRITTEN HISTORY

As the story goes, John Wilkes Booth was a famous actor and vehement supporter of the Southern cause. He also had a hatred for President Lincoln. On April 9, 1865, Confederate General Robert E. Lee surrendered to Union General Ulysses Grant at the Appomattox courthouse near Petersburg, Virginia, finally bringing to an end the conflict that cost our country over 650,000 deaths. Booth felt that by either kidnapping or killing the leaders of the North, the government would collapse. With the collapse of the government, the Confederacy could continue the fight. Before Lincoln was assassinated, on March 20, Booth and six conspirators actually attempted in April to kidnap President Lincoln. A change in plans prevented Lincoln from going to the spot of the attempted crime.

As the inevitable end to the war drew near, Booth gathered his group of co-conspirators, Lewis Powell, David Herold, and George Atzerodt. They discussed their plan and hid weapons in a boarding house owned by Mary Surratt near what is now Clinton, Maryland. When their original scheme to kidnap the President failed, the plan changed drastically. Booth decided that he now had to kill the President and other high-ranking members of the government. He plotted that Powell and Herold would kill Secretary of State William H. Seward, and Atzerodt would assassinate Vice President Andrew Johnson. Booth believed that upon the death of the leaders of the federal government, the citizens of the South would celebrate the assassins as heroes. Good Friday, April 14,

1865, was the date selected when it was learned that President Lincoln would attend Ford's Theatre with his wife and General Grant to watch the play *Our American Cousin*.

On the fateful day, Lincoln met with Grant at the White House, and, for some reason, the General told the President he would not be attending the play later that night. Since Julia and Ulysses Grant would not be attending, a young Army officer, Henry Rathbone, and his fiancé, Clara Harris, the daughter of New York Senator Ira Harris, were invited to attend with the President.

Lincoln occupied a private box above the stage with his wife Mary, Henry Rathbone, and Rathbone's fiancé. The presidential box was guarded by a single policeman, John Frederick Parker. During the intermission, the guard, and Lincoln's footman and coachman went to a tavern across the street leaving the box unguarded. Around 10:25 p.m., Booth entered the presidential box.

The assassin barricaded the booth from the inside and quietly approached the president. He fired a .44 caliber bullet from a single-shot Philadelphia derringer at point blank range into the back of Lincoln's head. The president slumped forward and his wife, Mary, screamed. Major Rathbone immediately rushed at Booth, but the killer stabbed the soldier in the shoulder. The actor-turned-murderer leapt from the box to the stage, approximately twelve feet below. His spur became tangled in the bunting that decorated the box and he landed heavily on his left foot, breaking his leg.

**John Wilkes Booth,
actor turned assassin.**
Courtesy US Archives.

**Ford's Theatre,
the scene of the Lincoln assassination.**
Courtesy Dollarphotoclub.

Presidential box at Ford's Theatre. The scene of the assassination.
Courtesy US Archives.

The .44-caliber Philadelphia Derringer. The weapon that killed President Lincoln.
Courtesy US Archives.

He shouted *Sic semper tyrannis!* ("Thus ever to tyrants!"—the Virginia state motto) as he landed on the stage. The crowd was slow to react thinking it was part of the play until they heard the hysterical screaming of Mary Todd Lincoln. Booth managed to exit the theatre and began his escape from Washington, DC, on horseback, riding over the Navy Yard bridge crossing the Anacostia River, the only way out of Washington that was not guarded by the military. David Herold escaped using the same route less than an hour later and met up with Booth at Mary Surratts' boarding house where they had hidden additional firearms. Keep in mind that both assassins used the only unguarded bridge out of the capital. One of the largest manhunts in history was now unleashed with over 10,000 federal troops, police, and detectives attempting to hunt down the well-known actor and his accomplishes.

Lincoln was carried from Ford's Theatre to a private home across the street. Secretary of War Edwin Stanton, who just happened to be nearby, entered the building and immediately took charge of the scene. He issued orders and instructions for the pursuit of Booth. Mary Lincoln and the children were not present at the time of the president's passing. The sixteenth president of the United States was pronounced dead at 7:22 a.m. on April 15, 1865. He was fifty-six years of age.

Lewis Powell and David Herold were assigned the assassination of Secretary of State William H. Seward, who had been badly injured in a carriage accident nine days earlier and was recovering at his home. Herold held Lewis Powell's horse while Powell entered the home of the secretary. Seward's son attempted to stop Powell. The would-be assassin attempted to kill the son, but his pistol misfired. The intruder hit the son over the head several times with his pistol and left him lying in a pool of blood. Powell gained access to the bedroom of Seward and began to stab him repeatedly in the neck and face. A military guard and nurse responded to the melee and forced the conspirator to leave the house. Herold heard the noise and screams from the building, panicked, and rode off with both horses leaving Powell to fend for himself. Powell somehow made his way to Mary Surratt's boarding house where he was captured the next day.

The popular historical version of the events states that George Atzerodt was assigned the job of executing Vice President Andrew Johnson. The would-be assassin rented a room at the same hotel occupied by the vice president. His assignment was to shoot Johnson at 10:15 p.m. to coincide with the other killings. But rather than following through with the plan, Atzerodt went to the bar, got drunk, and wandered through the streets of Washington and did not carry through with his part of the scheme. That night he did not return to the hotel occupied by the vice president but checked into another one. From there he made his way to his cousin's house in Germantown, Maryland, where he was eventually apprehended. He was not near any of the violent acts that occurred on the night of April 14. (As you will see, it may be more to it that there was no attack on Andrew Johnson.)

The manner in which Atzerodt was accused is quite interesting. An "employee" of the hotel reported a "suspicious looking man in a gray coat." When the police searched the room they found a loaded pistol under his pillow and a hidden Bowie knife. They also found a bank book belonging to John Wilkes

Booth. Atzerodt was arrested six days after the assassination at his cousin's house. Even though he did not actively participate in any act of violence, he was hung along with the active participants on July 7, 1865. He was tried and executed in less than two-and-one-half months after the killing of Lincoln. The new president, Andrew Johnson, pushed hard for a rapid trial and executions. There is a real possibility that Atzerodt was framed for the murder—the old *dead men tell no tales* thing.

Booth and Herold headed for Mary Surratts' boarding house located south of the capital in Maryland where they had stored firearms and supplies. The unexpected breaking of Booth's leg presented a problem, so he was taken to the home of Doctor Samuel Mudd. The physician set the assassin's leg and put it in a splint. He even constructed a pair of crutches for the patient. Booth and Herold spent a day at the house of the doctor before beginning their attempted escape to Virginia and what they thought would be a friendly population that would welcome them with open arms for killing Lincoln.

In spite of this massive manhunt, it was not until April 26, twelve days later, that federal cavalry from the 16th New York supposedly caught up with Booth and Herold at the Garret Farm in Virginia. Herold surrendered, but Booth was shot and killed by a sergeant named Boston Corbett in spite of orders to take Booth alive. (I think you can see where I am going with a second conspiracy.)

DEAD MEN AND WOMEN TELL NO TALES

Anyone associated with the assassins was arrested. The four main defendants were Surratt, Powell, Herold, and Atzerodt. Among the others arrested were Louis Weichmann, a friend of Mary Surratt's son and frequent resident at her boarding house. He was also a clerk for the War Department headed by Secretary Edwin Stanton. Dr. Samuel Mudd was arrested for giving medical care to Booth. Edmund Spangler, an employee at Ford's Theatre that held Booth's horse, Samuel Arnold, who was involved with the plan to kidnap Lincoln but dropped out before the assassination, and Michael O'Laughlen, an early conspirator in the kidnapping attempt, were also arrested.

The military tribunal lasted around six weeks. Since this was a military inquiry instead of a civil trial, the secretary of war controlled who acted as jurors. Weichmann, the friend of Mary Surratt's son and clerk who worked for Secretary of War Stanton, became the key witness for the prosecution in return for his freedom. Mary Surratt, Lewis Powell, David Herold, and George Atzerodt were sentenced to death by hanging. Samuel Mudd, Samuel Arnold, and Michael O'Laughlen were sentenced to life in prison. Edmund Spangler was sentenced to six years.

On July 7, 1865, Surratt, Powell, Herold, and Atzerodt were hung in the Old Arsenal Penitentiary. The owner of the boarding house became the first female

Hanging of the Conspirators:
Mary Surratt, Lewis Powell, David Herold, and George Atzerodt.
Courtesy US Archives.

ever executed by the federal government. After the sentencing, five of the jurors wrote a letter to President Johnson recommending that she not be hanged, but the president claimed he never saw the letter. Within three months of the assassination of Abraham Lincoln, all of the key witness that had knowledge of the crime were silenced forever.

O'Laughlen died in prison from yellow fever. In 1869, President Johnson, before leaving office, pardoned Mudd, Arnold, and Spangler after serving only four years of a life term. It is interesting to note that his term as president ended in 1869 after having undergone an impeachment by the Senate. His act of clemency was one of his last actions in office. Rumors of a great Lincoln conspiracy have been written about for over 150 years.

GENERAL GRANT CONFESSES

Ulysses S. Grant.
Courtesy Us Archives.

My first clue to the existence of a much larger conspiracy to kill Abraham Lincoln came during a channeling session in 2013. Any of you who have read my previous book, *Afterlife: What Really Happens on the Other Side: True Stories of Contact and Communication with Spirits*, chapter 13, An Interview with General Grant, you know that we spent several sessions with the spirit of former president of the United States Ulysses Grant. During those events, the general opened the door to additional investigation of the events of 1865.

In our original session, we were inquiring into whether Julia Grant and Mary Todd Lincoln liked each other. Grant's response to the inquiry was:

THEY DISLIKED ONE ANOTHER IN THE END.

As a follow up question, I'd asked why they did not like each other. His answer is what sparked this chapter.

MARY WAS JEALOUS OF JULIA. MARY WAS NOT RIGHT. I HAVE MY OWN SECRET. I WAS NOT A FAN OF MR. LINCOLN. THERE IS MORE. SINCE WE ARE MAKING CONFESSIONS, I WAS ASKED NOT TO GO TO FORD'S THEATRE.

That was certainly not the answer I had been expecting! I was aware that the Grants declined an invitation to attend Ford's Theatre but this was the first time I heard he was asked not to go.

THE TRUTH WILL SET YOU FREE

I knew the general was supposed to attend the theatre with the president and his wife, but I thought he had turned down the invitation because of a disagreement at a meeting with Lincoln the day of the assassination. Next, I asked him who told him not to go. There were very few individuals in Washington, DC, at the time that could give an order to the commander of the Army. His answer was evasive:

ON THAT I AM CONSIDERING WHETHER TO REVEAL AT THIS TIME.

Even on the other side, after 150 years, the general was unsure if he should confide the truth. I interjected: Did Julia tell you not to go? His reply was:

No.

THE PLOT THICKENS

He was still unsure if he could trust me with the information. The fact that only one major bridge out of the capital was unguarded would have been a military decision. I asked him if Secretary Stanton was the one who had ordered him not to go to the theatre. His answer showed he was still not certain if he should disclose the facts. It was:

MEMBERS OF COUNCIL IS ALL I WILL SAY.

Then he added:

BOOTH WAS HIRED.

The cat was starting to crawl out of the bag! My next question was obvious: Who hired Booth? He replied:

FOR THE RECORD I CANNOT ANY LONGER SUPPRESS THAT KNOWLEDGE. SECRETARY OF WAR.

Edwin Stanton, Lincoln's trusted secretary of war, was the mastermind behind the murder of the president! In researching this chapter, I had read conspiracy theories that Stanton was behind the assassination. General Grant had just verified the theories. I asked if he had accompanied the president to Ford's Theatre would the assassination have occurred on that night. He replied:

No.

I followed up with a statement: The day of the assassination there was a meeting at the White House. I inquired if the General had told Stanton at that meeting he was not going to accompany the President to the theatre. He replied:

YES.

I then asked if his not going to the theatre was the signal to go ahead with the plan. His answer was:

No, I DID NOT KNOW OF ANY SUCH PLAN.

I believe the general thought I was accusing him of participating in the plot to kill Lincoln. He wanted to make sure everyone knew there was no involvement on his part to kill the president. I read that Grant did not like the secretary of war. My next question inquired of his opinion of Stanton. To no one's surprise he replied:

He was an arrogant SOB. Lincoln was a progressive.

The General was very plain spoken in life and being on the other side did little to clean up his language. Apparently, the secretary of war chose his conspirators carefully. The commanding general of the Army would not have been approachable on the subject of killing the president.

If the conspiracy was as far reaching as I was beginning to suspect, there must have been a large group of individuals involved. My next question was who all was involved. Grant's reply was:

His cabinet.

I asked if there were many involved, and his answer was:

Yes.

Did you realize what had happened after the deed was done and Lincoln was dead? His reply was:

Yes, we all did after the act.

DESTROYING THE EVIDENCE

Before Robert Todd Lincoln, the son of Mary Todd and Abraham Lincoln, died in 1926, he turned many of the family documents over to the Library of Congress. Philip Van Doren Stern published a book titled *The Man Who Killed Lincoln*, in which he states that a friend saw Robert Todd Lincoln burning papers in a fireplace. Lincoln was supposed to have said that the letters contained evidence of treason by members of his father's cabinet. I asked the spirit of General Grant if those letters contained evidence pertaining to the assassination. His reply was:

Yes, too many were involved.

When the documents were released to the public in 1947, no mention was made of the conspiracy.

As we ended the interview with the spirit of Ulysses Grant, I asked him if he wanted the world to know the facts concerning the death of Abraham Lincoln. His reply was:

It is what it is.

I took from that statement that I had his approval to publish this information. As the session ended, I decided to pursue additional information concerning the Lincoln conspiracy.

One evening, in October 2013, I made up a list of questions concerning the Lincoln conspiracy and requested a master guide that could answer my inquiries. On that particular night, our guide was Thomas. He had visited us before and provided amazing information. I started the session by asking if he knew what my questions were for the night. His reply was:

BASICALLY.

Once again the guides knew what was on my mind and responded with a guide capable of answering the questions.

GRANT'S TESTIMONY VERIFIED

I thought I would start out by confirming information about Ulysses Grant's role, if any, in the conspiracy. I asked if the commanding general of the Army knew anything about the plan to assassinate Lincoln before the event took place, and the answer was:

NO.

I then inquired if Secretary of War Stanton had told Grant not to go to Ford's Theatre with the Lincolns. His reply was:

YES.

The information the guide provided backed up everything that had been told to us by Grant's spirit in our earlier session. My next question was asked if Secretary of War Edwin Stanton was behind the Lincoln conspiracy. There was no hesitation as he answered:

YES.

Secretary of War Edwin Stanton. Chief planner of the Lincoln assassination.
Courtesy US Archives.

It also was verification once again of what we had been told in our prior session. I followed up by seeking the names of the cabinet members involved. His reply was a bit evasive:

ONLY A FEW.

Vice President Andrew Johnson was a member of the cabinet and was only sworn in as vice president six weeks before the killing of President Lincoln. I inquired if he was involved and the guide replied:

YES.

Lincoln's own vice president had helped plan his murder! Before being picked to run with Lincoln in 1864, Andrew Johnson had acted as the Military Governor of Tennessee, a position to which he was appointed in 1862. Prior to

**President Andrew Johnson,
a co-conspirator in the Lincoln
assassination.**
Courtesy US Archives.

that appointment, he had served in the US Senate where he became aware of the inner workings in the capital. His choice as the pick to run with Lincoln came as a bit of a surprise to political insiders of the era.

Since Johnson's appointment as military governor of Tennessee was a military position, he would have had contact with Secretary of War Stanton. Stanton remained in his position after Johnson took office but differed with the new president over the issue of giving voting rights to former slaves. Ironically, the impeachment of Johnson took place over his attempt to remove Stanton from his cabinet.

I would like to digress for a moment and refer to the upcoming Chapter 13, Killing Camelot, where you will find that Vice President Lyndon Johnson was a co-conspirator in the murder of John Kennedy. I think the message here is that if you are president of the United States, you should never have a vice president named "Johnson."

Getting back to the channeling session, there are theories that other institutions were involved in the plan. I asked if there were any high-ranking members of the Confederacy involved and the reply was:

No.

It was rumored at the time that members of the Catholic church were part of the conspiracy? His answer to that question was once again:

No.

The killing of Abraham Lincoln was a home-grown conspiracy directed by high-ranking members of our own government.

John Wilkes Booth was given access to the unguarded box at Ford's Theatre because the armed guard had gone to a bar across the street and was not guarding the president. I asked why the guard was not present and the answer was:

HE WAS CALLED AWAY.

So the guard was called away from his post so the crime could take place? The message from the guide was:

YES, BUT HE DID NOT KNOW.

Our guide clarified that the policeman that was to guard the box was an unknowing accomplice. When I asked if Stanton provided an escape route for Booth the answer was:

THERE WAS A PLAN.

It was becoming obvious the unguarded bridge at the Naval Yard was no accident. As mentioned, Mary Surratt, the owner of the boarding house that was the rallying point for the conspirators, was the first female ever hung by the Federal government. I asked if she was guilty. Our guide answered:

YES.

No woman had ever been hung in US military history. When I asked why they hung her the answer was:

SHE HARBORED THE ACCOMPLICES.

Keep in mind that the new President Johnson was given a petition by the jurors to save her life but claimed he did not see the letter. Mary Surratt certainly knew too much about who was behind the conspiracy.

Dr. Mudd set Booth's leg and allowed the conspirators to remain in his house for a day. At his military trial the jurors actually voted 4-5 against him being hanged with the four main conspirators. He was sentenced to life in prison but pardoned by President Johnson. When I asked if he was involved with the plan to kill Lincoln the answer was:

NO.

History records that Dr. Mudd was aware that Booth had assassinated the president while he gave him medical assistance. The guide replied that he was aware that his patient had perpetrated the crime. I guess President Johnson pardoned him since he was aware of who really was responsible for the murder of Lincoln.

THE JOHN WILKES BOOTH CONSPIRACY

And now for the second part of the conspiracy. According to history, Booth and David Herold slipped out of Washington and went to the home of Dr. Samuel Mudd where the doctor set Booth's leg that was broken when he landed on the stage of Ford's Theatre. The pair of assassins hid in barns and swamps as they made their way south through Maryland. Eventually they borrowed a rowboat, crossed the Potomac River and entered Virginia. They supposedly hid in a barn on the Richard Garrett farm, located approximately three miles south of what is now Port Royal, Virginia.

Acting on a tip, the 16th New York Cavalry surrounded the Garret tobacco barn in which Herold and Booth were hiding. Herold surrendered, but Booth refused to give up. The barn was set on fire in an effort to drive Booth out.

In spite of orders to take Booth alive, Sgt. Boston Corbett fired a single shot through a crack in the barn that hit Booth in the neck at the base of the head. Booth is said to have died several hours later, and his body was taken to Washington. All of the events surrounding Booth's death were under the command of Secretary Stanton.

During a channeling session, I asked the guide if John Wilkes Booth was killed in the barn in rural Virginia. As you can probably guess by now, the answer was:

No.

My next question was who was really killed by the cavalry Sergeant and the guide said:

A worker, farmhand.

In order to authenticate the information that we were receiving, I asked the guide the tough question: What was Booth's assumed name after he made his escape? The guide answered:

John St. Helen.

This answer supported a theory that Booth actually escaped to Franklin County, Tennessee, and assumed the name John St. Helen. Ben Chitty, a historian at the University of the South, collected evidence that Booth married a Sewanee woman named Louisa Payne in 1872. The physical evidence he based his assumption on was an entry in the marriage records at the courthouse that bore the signature "Jno. W. Booth." The couple lived under the name St. Helen, but she required that they be married under his real name.

In 1926, the son of Louisa Payne gave an interview in which he told of overhearing his stepfather tell his mother about knots on his left leg and admit that he was Booth. He said that Booth/St. Helen threatened to "rip his throat from ear to ear" if he ever told anyone about what he'd overheard. Several months later, Booth abandoned the Paynes, with no regard for her being pregnant, and headed to Texas.

John St. Helen settled in Glen Rose, Texas, for a short period of time where he owned a store. One evening he learned that a local girl was going to marry a US marshal. Realizing the arrival of the lawman was bad news, and he would probably be recognized by the federal agent, he abandoned his store and headed for Granbury, Texas, on the same night the marshal arrived in town.

Booth/St. Helen lived in Granbury where he tended bar at two different saloons. He resided on the Texas frontier for several years where he made the acquaintance of a Tennessee attorney named Finis Bates. At the time, Bates suspected that John St. Helen really was Booth but failed to act on his hunch. Everything went well for St. Helen in Granbury until he became sick and thought he was going to die. On what he thought was his death bed, he confessed

JOHN WILKES BOOTH, AGED 64.
(11 Days After Death.) In the Morgue at Enid, Much
Swollen From the Poison He Had Taken.

John Wilkes Booth in his casket, Enid, Oklahoma, 1903.
Courtesy US Archives.

John Wilkes Booth's mummified body.
Courtesy bothiebarn.files.com.

to being John Wilkes Booth, the killer of President Lincoln. Fortunately—or unfortunately—he survived the illness.

As soon as his health allowed, he left Texas and headed for Enid, Oklahoma, where he changed his name to David E. George and worked at odd jobs. In 1903, a dying alcoholic house painter confessed to a minister in that town that he was John Wilkes Booth. This time it really was a dying confession. The photo **above** shows Booth, eleven days after he died in his casket. According to the caption on the photograph, the assassin that killed President Lincoln finally took his own life by swallowing poison.

A SHOWMAN AFTER DEATH

If you think the story is weird up to now, hold on to your hat. Finis Bates who had known St. Helen decades earlier and suspected he was John Wilkes Booth, learned of the death of George/Booth, traveled to Oklahoma, and identified the body as the individual he had known earlier as John St. Helens. Bates acquired the body and had it preserved, i.e., mummified. After Bates died, his widow sold the body to a carnival where it became a side-show attraction. It is fitting that John Wilkes Booth, the great actor, remained a center of attraction for many years after his death. His body was even on display at the 1904 St. Louis World's Fair.

Additional evidence that the mummy really was John Wilkes Booth appeared when a *Life* magazine article in 1931 showed that six doctors in Chicago examined the preserved body. They also x-rayed the remains. Their findings indicated a shorter left leg, a distorted right thumb, and a scar on the neck that were consistent with physical characteristics of the conspirator who had supposedly died in 1865. The mummified body was last reported seen at a carnival in Pennsylvania in the 1970s. There is a distinct possibility the body of John Wilkes Booth still exists and that DNA could answer the question of his survival once and for all. For my part, I will accept the words of the master guide, who gave me the name of John St. Helen and information that the escape of Booth was all part of a well-planned conspiracy.

As I mentioned earlier, President Andrew Johnson pardoned the conspirators who were to serve life sentences before he left office. I asked the guide why he'd issued the pardons. His answer put the nail in the coffin as to what really took place. He said:

BECAUSE HE WAS ONE OF THEM.

It appears that then-President Johnson issued pardons in return for their continued silence. The spirits on the other side have no doubt that Andrew Johnson was a co-conspirator in the death of Abraham Lincoln.

Abraham Lincoln was going to facilitate the rebuilding of the South and possibly even give voting rights to the former slaves. Secretary of War Edwin Stanton, along with Vice President Andrew Johnson and other members of his cabinet, formulated a complex plan to assassinate Abraham Lincoln. John Wilkes Booth was a famous actor with a love for the South and a deep hatred for the president and was quite willing to participate in the plan. The secretary of war was in a position to manipulate the search for the conspirators and assure their escape.

The captured conspirators were given a speedy trial before a military tribunal, once again under the influence of Edwin Stanton. Those most familiar with the facts were almost immediately hung to assure their silence. John Wilkes Booth escaped and a story was concocted that he was killed. He went west and lived into the twentieth century. While many historians will disagree with this interpretation of the events surrounding the killing of Abraham Lincoln, I believe the spirits wanted the truth to be known and this is their version of what happened. When I started writing this chapter, I never thought it was going to be a double conspiracy. ∞

CHAPTER 3

THE SECRET BEHIND

ALIEN SECRECY

Perhaps one of the greatest conspiracies of modern times is that of the governments of the world attempting to keep the truth about aliens from the population. We have seen examples of the extreme measures practiced by our government in the Roswell incident and by the United Kingdom during and after the Rendlesham Forest Lights occurrence. In this chapter I rely heavily on channeling sessions with our alien friend, Mou (see my prior book *Aliens Among Us: Past and Present*). He has provided us with an incredible amount of information about a lot of subjects. In fact, he recommended that I write this chapter.

Measures to keep the secret can actually be quite severe. When I asked Mou if anyone was killed to keep the secret of Rendlesham Forest incident in Great Britain his answer was:

HA, HA, HA, HA!

Obviously, he thought it was a laughable question. When I asked him why he was laughing, his answer was:

IT WAS AGAINST YOUR AGREEMENTS. HAVE OTHER WAYS THEY WERE TOLD TO USE.

Notice that he indicated more than one agreement. His answer opened the door to a lot of questions concerning the interactions of world governments and extraterrestrials. In order to have more than one agreement, we must have been communicating with them for quite a while. When I asked who was the first president to make contact with extraterrestrials, I was not prepared for his answer.

WASHINGTON.

Mou has been known to pull my leg with his answers. I suspected this was one of those instances. I asked: Are you saying that all of our presidents communicated with aliens?

NO, SOME REFUSED US.

When I asked who the first president was that made a treaty, his answer surprised me.

I DO NOT KNOW MY HISTORY WELL BUT EARLY 1800S. AFTER WASHINGTON. CLOSE...HE DIED EARLY. LIKE NUMBER 10.

My guess is he meant William Henry Harrison, the ninth president, who died after only thirty-two days in office, April 1841. I hope dealing with the aliens was not so traumatic it caused his death. That answer really caught me off guard! My reply was: "Are you saying all of our presidents have had contacts with aliens?"

BASICALLY TRUE.

In my research, I've found that extraterrestrial interaction with our presidents was not uncommon. Harry Truman even went for a ride on one of their vessels.

THE COMMITTEE

We had been told before that there is a governing committee that controls the actions of the advanced cultures in our galaxy. Since ours is a much younger culture here on earth, the committee has to protect us from more advanced societies that could easily conquer humans. Our visitors from outer space must have amazing technology to travel the stars. They must also have amazing weapons! I asked if extraterrestrials ever fought each other.

WE DID AT ONE TIME. THIS IS WHY THE COMMITTEE WAS FORMED. NOW THERE IS NOT MUCH DISAGREEMENT.

In his next statement he went on to give us more detail.

IN ALL THE UNIVERSES, THOSE WHO HAVE THE ABILITY TO WHAT WE CALL "SKIP TRAVEL," OR TRAVEL THROUGH WORM HOLES, HAVE THREE MEMBERS WHO SIT THE COUNCIL. WE WATCH ALL THAT HAPPENS. YOU HAVE TO FOLLOW THE LAWS SET DOWN. THIS COUNCIL IS VERY OLD AND WAS ESTABLISHED TO PROTECT PLANETS LIKE YOURS FROM INVASION.

If the answer to becoming an advanced culture is to live together with little disagreement, humans really have a long way to go! When I asked him to explain how the Galaxy was governed he said:

ADVANCED PLACES ARE GOVERNED BY A COMMITTEE. WE HAVE TO GET THE OK TO PLAY ON THE PLANETS WITH LIFE.

Are you saying that all extraterrestrials have to get permission to visit Earth?

ALL HAVE TO GO THRU THE INTER-PLANET COMMITTEE TO VISIT. WE ARE NOT FREE TO INTERFERE.

I have this mental image of aliens lining up to get tickets to visit Earth, a lot like us going to the local zoo to observe the animals. I know the temptation to interfere with humans must be very great. My next question was, How does the committee know if anyone breaks the rules?

WE HAVE DEVICES LIKE CAMERAS. THEY MUST CARRY AT ALL TIMES. SO AN ALARM GOES OFF IF SOMEONE BREAKS A RULE. IF YOU CHOOSE TO VISIT A PLANET YOU AGREE TO FOLLOW PROTOCOL. THIS DEVICE MONITORS YOUR FEELINGS.

So they know if you are even thinking about breaking the rules. For the system to work efficiently, there must be penalties if the rules are broken. When I inquired about what happened when rules were broken, he said:

THEY ARE PUNISHED BY SANCTIONS AND EXPELLED UNTIL THEY PAY BACK THE COMMITTEE WITH GIFTS FOR ALL THE PLANETS. A COSTLY MISTAKE. YOURS IS NOT THE ONLY PLANET WE HAVE RESTRICTIONS ON. THERE ARE THOUSANDS.

It is hard to imagine the scope of the power of the committee and number of planets over which they have power. It is with this committee that the governments of earth have negotiated a treaty. It is the fear of the repercussions of breaking this treaty that have caused the governing bodies to go to such great lengths to keep the presence of aliens a secret.

THE TREATY

In previous channeling sessions we talked about the fact that there was a treaty made among the major governments of the world and the extraterrestrials. I asked him the basic terms of the treaty.

YOU AGREED NOT TO TELL ABOUT US. TO LET US WALK AMONG YOU. DO STUDIES ON YOU AND TO DO OUR OWN MANIPULATION. THERE IS A LOT MORE I CANNOT TELL YOU.

It is becoming apparent why such a treaty is being kept a secret. The officials of governments have given the aliens permission to perform abductions and whatever their "own manipulation" is. Such news would surely not go over well with voters.

He had told me before that the information given me was "dumbed down" for my protection. As I asked my questions, I could not help but think about him laughing when I asked if anyone was killed to keep the secrets. When I attempted to delve deeper into the content of the treaty, he said:

WE WILL LET YOU ALONE IF YOU LET US WATCH. YOU HAVE TO REMEMBER THAT WE HAVE BEEN HERE SINCE THREE MANLIKE ANIMALS ROAMED THE PLANET. WE WATCHED YOUR LAST ICE AGE. WE HAVE LET YOUR PLANET EVOLVE WITH ONLY TWO OR THREE MAJOR INTRUSIONS.

I have visions of a written agreement, something like the treaties we make with other countries. I asked if there is a written agreement.

IT IS ON A HANDSHAKE, NOT WRITTEN.

If it is based on a handshake, the aliens must keep a very close watch. There are few of our politicians who can be trusted with a handshake agreement. For this to work, the people in the know must really be afraid of extraterrestrial retaliation. I thought I would ask what the committee thinks of our current President, Obama. Once again, I am delivering the words of our guide, not my own.

I CARE NOT FOR HIS HONESTY TOWARD THE PEOPLE. HE CANNOT TELL NON TRUTHS TO THE COMMITTEE SO HE DOES NOT SPEAK TO THEM. SO RIGHT NOW THE USA IS NOT IN CONTACT WITH THEM. THUS OTHER COUNTRIES ARE ADVANCING BEYOND YOU.

As you can see, contact with the committee is not just an American phenomenon. Other countries seem to be in constant contact with the visitors from other planets. If the countries of earth gave them permission to study and manipulate the population of our Planet, hopefully, we got something in return. When I asked what we received as our part of the treaty, he replied:

I AM NOT VERSED IN THIS AS MUCH AS I SHOULD BE, BUT I KNOW WE SENT AN ADVISOR TO TEACH YOUNG SCIENTISTS ABOUT ATOM SPLITTING. YOU FIGURED OUT HYDROGEN. YOU MADE A BOMB, AND YOU WERE WARNED NOT TO. YOU SET IT OFF AND JUST ABOUT DESTROYED EARTH. WE HAD TO STOP IT. WE VOLUNTEERED KNOWING ABOUT GENES. AND WE HELPED UNDERSTAND STEALTH.

In return for us letting the aliens treat earth like a petting zoo and experimental laboratory, we are given information to help advance our civilization. It also appears that when we tested a hydrogen bomb against their advice, they had to step in to save our planet. When you phrase it like that, I guess it sounds like a pretty good deal.

GOVERNMENT FEAR OF THE TRUTH

It is obvious the governments of the earth go to great extremes to keep the existence of extraterrestrials a secret. The treaty is one reason, but when I asked the main reason for the secrecy, he replied:

FEARS. TODAY PEOPLE RUN ON FEAR. LOOK WHAT OCCURRED WHEN ON THE RADIO, A PLAY CAME ON ABOUT ALIENS ATTACKING. JUST A PLAY, AND PEOPLE KILLED THEMSELVES. IT WAS KIND OF A TEST TO SEE WHAT YOU MIGHT DO. WELL, WE ALL KNOW ONLY THE CRAZY BELIEVE IN GHOSTS AND ALIENS.

He was referring to the Orson Welles radio broadcast, the *War of the Worlds*, on October 30, 1938, when many citizens were convinced that an invasion was taking place from the inhabitants of Mars. It created a mass hysteria and some even committed suicide. Having written about extraterrestrial interactions at places like the Nazca lines in Peru, I asked how early humans viewed the visitors.

IN TIMES BEFORE, THE PEOPLE SAW US AS GOOD NEWS. A VISIT FROM GOD. AFTER WE TOLD THEM WE WERE NOT GODS, WE STILL REMAINED GODS, OR MEN FROM THE HEAVENS.

Something apparently happened to the opinions of the inhabitants of earth through the centuries. Ancient man viewed the extraterrestrials as friends but our modern civilizations fear them. I asked our alien guide what happened to so radically change the opinions of the inhabitants of our planet. He replied:

FEAR, POWER, GREED.

As the human race advanced so did the ability of the inhabitants to achieve more power. As with the advance of power, greed also grew. In order to achieve power and greed, fear becomes the tool of the powerful. As long as the people fear the visitors from other planets, the general population will not be able to learn the positive messages from the extraterrestrials. ∞

THE DEVIL'S VORTEXES, LEY LINES,

AND THE BERMUDA TRIANGLE

Throughout recorded history, certain areas of the earth have been deemed more dangerous than others. Some of these areas are referred to by many names, such as triangles or Devil's vortexes. In order to be a triangle there have to be intersecting lines. Vortexes are formed by the intersection of lines of energy, referred to as ley lines, that intersect at various places on earth. These energy lines were known to the ancients as they exploited them in their construction projects. As I researched these vortexes on the Internet, it seemed like there was a general consensus that there were twelve major vortexes around the world. When I asked Mou how many there really were, his answer was:

MORE LIKE 23.

That was a lot more than I expected. In order to attempt to understand these vortexes, it is first necessary to address an understanding of just what intersects to create these areas of energy.

LEY LINES

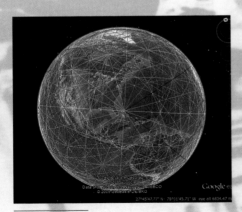

World ley lines and the Bermuda intersection.
Courtesy Google Earth & B. Hagens UVG grid.

Conceptually, the theory of global energy lines predates Egyptian cultures. In ancient Egypt, such lines were utilized to lay out the city of Cairo, dating to approximately 6,000 BC. Plato, Pythagoras, DaVinci, and many of the great thinkers attempted to define the concept. During the 1970s, Bethe Hagens and William Becker advanced the research to the point that they produced a series of grid maps that show the main intersection points of the energy lines. The image on the left shows an overlay of the Hagens ley line network superimposed on a Google Earth map. This view clearly shows the intersection point that forms the Bermuda Triangle. Voluminous research has been done on the subject of ley lines; if the reader would like to pursue the subject further, I have listed appropriate websites at the end of the chapter.

During the preparation of this chapter, I attempted to familiarize myself with the appropriate research in these areas. After becoming totally confused, I decided to approach the subject with our alien guide, Mou. One evening during a channeling session I asked if there really were mysterious forces within the Devil's triangles. His reply gave me enough incentive to write this chapter:

VERY MUCH, YES.

He went on to say:

THESE ARE LEY LINE INTERSECTIONS. SOMETIMES THEY HAPPEN NATURALLY, AND PEOPLE GET CAUGHT IN IT AND GO WHERE THE LAST ET TRAVELED TO.

I am not sure where the last ET traveled to, but I don't think it is good to go there. Whatever takes place in these areas, it is the result of natural phenomena. Earlier our spirit guide had mentioned that there were ley line intersections. I asked just what a ley line really was.

IT IS A NATURAL MAGNETIC LINE THAT DIVIDES THE EARTH. IT IS LIKE A RANGE THAT ALLOWS THE EARTH TO EXPAND AND CONTRACT LIKE SHE IS BREATHING. WHEN SHE IS BREATHING IN OR OUT THIS PRODUCES ENERGY. IF THE LINE CREATES AN ENERGY, THEN YOU CAN HARNESS THIS TO MOVE IN TIME AND SPACE. THIS CAN BE MANIPULATED.

What is the effect of a ley line?

PROVIDE PATHWAYS FOR ENERGY DISBURSEMENT.

I was having a little trouble understanding the disturbances were being caused by the earth breathing. When I asked again what causes the magnetic disturbances, he said:

NATURAL MAGNETIC PHENOMENON. SOME KNOW HOW TO USE THEM. ALL IS UNIVERSAL LAWS AND YOU WILL LEARN HOW TO USE THEM WHEN YOU LEARN THE MATH.

Had I mentioned recently that mankind has an awful lot to learn? Scientifically, you will find very little recognition that the ley lines actually exist. Proponents of the existence of ley lines will tell you that the intersection points are some of the most dangerous locations on the planet. You will also find that some of the most important sites, such as henges, pyramids, the Nazca Lines in Peru, and many of the famous megaliths are located along these lines. It seems as though the ancients were well aware of increases in the earth's energy and took advantage of it.

In the Middle Ages, scientists of the time attempted to locate these energy lines with dowsing rods. If these lines of energy do indeed exist, it is not hard to visualize that places where multiple lines intersect would be areas of extraordinary energy. As you can see, much research has been conducted through the years concerning the location of such high energy lines.

THE BERMUDA TRIANGLE

Perhaps the best known location of unknown energies is the Bermuda Triangle. A huge area in the shape of a triangle extending from Bermuda to Puerto Rico to Miami, it encompasses almost 500,000 square miles. Within this area there have been numerous mysterious happenings. Planes and ships have disappeared, never to be seen or heard from again, while in this vast area of the Atlantic Ocean. There are many scientific explanations, such as hidden reefs and sudden storms that would account for the strange disappearances hypothecated through the years.

Bermuda Triangle ley lines.
Courtesy Google Earth & B. Hagens UVG grid.

The image on the left shows a close up of the intersection of multiple ley lines just off the shore of Bimini, the heart of the area known as the Bermuda Triangle. If you look at various Internet sites, you see a lot of conjecture that aliens are the reason for the mysterious disappearances in this large area of the Atlantic Ocean. I thought I would find out right away if this chapter should be included in my books, so I asked Mou if extraterrestrials had anything to do with the mysteries of the Bermuda Triangle. His answer was:

No, NATURAL.

Whatever the causes, there are many documented instances of mysterious disappearances in the Bermuda Triangle. I will take time to discuss a few of the disappearances.

THE LOST SQUADRON
AND RESCUE AIRCRAFT

An incident occurring in 1945 is probably the greatest mystery associated with the triangle. On December 5, 1945, a sunny day at time of takeoff but with a storm front coming in, five US Navy Avenger torpedo-bombers with a total crew of fourteen took off from Ft. Lauderdale, Florida, on a routine training mission known as Flight 19, intended to last three hours. The squadron leader was

**Navy Avenger torpedo-bomber,
type of aircraft that disappeared.**
Courtesy Dollarphotoclub.

**US Navy Mariner Aircraft,
type of aircraft that disappeared
while looking for lost flight.**
Courtesy US Archives.

Lieutenant Robert F. Cox, an experienced military pilot who had been flying in the area for the past six months. Several hours into the flight, a radio message was received stating that his compass and backup compass had failed, and his position was unknown. It has to be assumed that the compasses on the other four planes would have also failed or at least one of the five pilots would have known their location. All attempts to find the location of the lost squadron failed. Around 6:20 in the evening a garbled message was heard from the Lieutenant calling for his men to simultaneously ditch their airplanes because of lack of fuel. This message was the last information ever known about Flight 19. In spite of a massive air and sea search, no evidence of bodies or wreckage were ever found. Rescue crews were immediately dispatched to the general vicinity.

As part of the air and sea rescue attempt, a Mariner aircraft holding a thirteen-man crew took off at 7:27 p.m. to search an area north of the Bahamas. Three minutes into the flight, the rescue ship radioed the base that they had begun their search mission. That was the last communication ever heard from the Mariner and its crew. A tanker, the *Gaines Mill*, off the coast of Florida, later reported seeing an explosion around 7:50 p.m. of the same evening. The navy was able to verify that the explosion viewed by the tanker was indeed the *Martin Mariner*. A carrier in the area, the USS *Solomons*, had been tracking the *Mariner* and saw the blip fall from the screen. In the case of the rescue aircraft, the navy knew exactly where the incident occurred.

In spite of having a fix on the location of the *Mariner*'s explosion, once again there was no trace of bodies or wreckage. Six military aircraft and twenty-seven men lost their lives without a trace in spite of the fact that hundreds of ships and aircraft participated in the search. One would also think that if a freighter had seen an explosion and a carrier recorded it on radar, it would have narrowed the area of the search and increased the odds of finding at least the remains of the *Mariner*.

During one of our sessions, I started off by inquiring if the Bermuda Triangle was one of the most dangerous places on earth. His reply was:

OH YES.

Next, I asked what caused the crash of the torpedo bombers. His reply was:

THE FORCE OF THE WATER.

Sometimes his answers are a bit obvious! I thought I would attempt another line of questioning. I inquired if their compasses were messed up by the natural magnetic forces of the vortex. He replied:

YES.

I asked what happened to the *Mariner* rescue airplane that disappeared while searching for the torpedo bombers.

MAGNETIC SHIFT. AFFECTS OLDER INSTRUMENTATION.

Now we were getting somewhere. My next question inquired if the planes ran out of gas.

NO.

Is it possible that Flight 19 flew into some type of anomaly or possibly a wormhole?

YES.

Did the wormhole take them too far from land for them to make it back?

NO, IT TOOK THEM INTO WHAT WOULD BE YOUR FUTURE.

He caught me off guard with that answer. I followed up by asking if they were moved to a future time. He replied:

WHAT'S CONSIDERED YOUR FUTURE?

I hate it when he answers a question with another question that I cannot answer. Maybe, if I restated it, I could get a straight answer. What year in the future were they moved to?

TIME IS ONLY YOUR TERM. HERE, TIME IS NOT LINEAR.

I have no idea what he is referring to by saying time is not linear. I asked if Flight 19 would ever reappear in our dimension at a future time. He replied:

OUTSIDE YOUR DIMENSION.

When I asked my alien guide, Mou, what happened to the twenty-seven men who were aboard the military aircraft, I received a much unexpected answer:

WE HAVE THEM.

I must admit that was the last answer I was expecting. When I asked him to clarify that he was saying they were still alive he answered:

YES.

You are saying that aliens are holding them captive?

ON A DIFFERENT DIMENSION.

So when people or objects disappear, you simply put them into another dimension?

YES.

When I asked him the purpose of sending the men to another dimension, his reply was:

KARMA.

I certainly can't argue with that answer, whatever he meant.

From my research, it seems like the Bermuda vortex must be one of the most dangerous places on earth. He had a different opinion:

MIDDLE EAST.

Can't disagree with that answer either!

A REAL TIME TRAVELER

Perhaps the best example of time travel in the Bermuda Triangle took place on December 4, 1970, when a young pilot named Bruce Gernon attempted to fly his Beechcraft Bonanza A36 from Andros Island to Palm Beach, Florida. At the time of the flight, the pilot had over 600 hours of flying experience and had flown this route more than a dozen times. He was accompanied on the flight by his father and a business associate.

Shortly after takeoff, they encountered a rapidly building cumulus cloud directly in his flight path. He attempted to out-climb the cloud and finally broke free at around 11,000 feet. As they approached Bimini, there was a huge storm cloud formation in front of them that appeared to rise to 60,000 feet, well above the capabilities of the Beechcraft. They had no choice but to enter the cloud. Upon entering, they found the cloud to be black and dark but without rain or lightning. What they did find was unusual bright white flashes that were growing in intensity.

As they attempted to get out of the strange cloud, the pilot noticed a U-shaped opening that was rapidly closing to form a type of tunnel in the cloud. Unfortunately, the opening appeared to be shrinking in size as they entered. The end of the tunnel appeared to be about a mile away and light reflected off the walls of the tunnel. In a matter of seconds, the Beechcraft exited the tunnel that closed behind them to form a slit-like cloud. By this time, all of the navigational gear was not functioning properly, and the magnetic compass was slowly spinning.

Upon exiting the opening in the clouds, they realized that they were flying through a grayish-white haze with limited visibility without any navigational equipment. A couple of minutes later, the Miami tower notified the pilot that it had located an airplane over Miami Beach. Gernon notified the tower that it had to be another airplane since he was just approaching the island of Bimini, which is ninety miles southwest of Miami. The cloud suddenly cleared and the pilot was able to see Miami Beach below them.

When he landed at Palm Beach, the entire elapsed time for the flight was less than forty-seven minutes. In order for him to have covered that distance, his Beechcraft, with a top speed or 230 miles per hour, would have had to travel at over three times the speed of sound. He had traveled approximately 100 miles in three minutes! In addition, he had only burned twenty-nine gallons of fuel when the trip usually consumed eighty gallons. This is probably the best documented instance of an individual traveling through a time warp.

After hearing the story for the first time, I thought it deserved its own channeling session. Mou was more than happy to supply the answers to what had taken place. I started by asking if Bruce Gernon had undergone his famous flight as publicized. He replied:

INDEED. NOT MYSTICAL SCIENCE TO USE YOUR TERMS.

I had read that some thought there might have been an extraterrestrial involvement. When I inquired if it was part of an alien abduction, he said:

NO, NOT ALIEN.

We've had long discussions in the past about travel in wormholes, so I asked if this was an example of what happens when an airplane gets caught in a wormhole.

YES.

What makes such a wormhole form?

INCREASED FREQUENCY OF ELECTROMAGNETIC CHARGE.

Where does the energy come from to form a wormhole?

WITHIN YOUR OWN ATMOSPHERE.

What makes it form?

YOUR EARTH POSITION.

In an effort to better understand what he was saying, I asked what earth position makes a wormhole easier to form. He replied:

PLACEMENT WITHIN ITS GALAXY WHILE WITHIN CERTAIN CONDITIONS.

Enhanced conditions such as a thunderstorm.

That made a lot of sense; Gernon was flying into some very strange cloud formations. I thought I would try to expand on this line of questioning and asked how it was formed.

I just explained in your terms.

His answer was a clear hint that he had already answered the question and was ready to move on. I thought I would change the subject, so I inquired if this could only happen in a vortex such as the Bermuda Triangle. He replied:

Stronger possibility within certain locations.

What happens when you enter a wormhole?

There is no measure of your time. Opportunity to expand.

From that answer, I surmise that when you enter a wormhole, time as we know it ceases to exist. He made a few more comments that also complicated the subject.

Time is only your term. Here time is not linear.

Definitely time to change the subject. I stated that he mentioned flying through a white fog. Bruce Gernon and Rob McGregor published a book entitled *The Fog* in which they discuss the presence of an "electronic fog." When I asked Mou to describe the white fog, he said:

Dense electromagnetic energy.

Is this type of event common?

Not so much.

Was the Beechcraft ever in any danger?

No, fortunate.

The events described by Bruce Gernon are real and give us a look at the mysterious natural phenomena that occurs in the energy vortexes of the world. For those of you who think time travel is not possible, I would suggest that a vacation within the confines of the Bermuda Triangle should not be in your future.

DISAPPEARANCE OF THE USS *CYCLOPS*

The USS *Cyclops* was a naval vessel utilized for the transportation of bulk cargo. In the early 1900s, most of our ships burned coal, and this was one of the vessels designed to transport heavy materials. It departed Rio de Janerio on February 15, 1918, loaded with approximately 11,000 tons of Magnesium ore, headed for Baltimore, Maryland. On March 3, she made an unscheduled stop in Barbados. On March 4, the ship departed Barbados with 306 crew members and passengers, heading into the Bermuda Triangle, never to be seen again. To date, there has been no evidence of the remains of the ship or passengers ever found. What happened to the USS *Cyclops* remains one of the great mysteries in naval history.

I thought the best way to solve the mystery of the loss of the USS *Cyclops* would be to ask our spirit guides. One evening I asked our guide what happened to the missing naval vessel. He replied.

Photo #: 19-N-13451   USS Cyclops on 3 Oct. 1911

USS *Cyclops*, US naval vessel lost in Bermuda Triangle.
Courtesy US Archives.

SURGES ARE COMMON IN VORTEX. CAN INFLUENCE MANY WEATHER EVENTS.

Are you saying that an energy surge in the Bermuda Triangle vortex caused the sinking of the USS *Cyclops* with all the crew and passengers on board?

YES.

What happens when a ship is caught in one of these magnetic vortexes?

DRAWN TOWARD THE APEX.

Is it like a whirlpool in the ocean?

NO.

Can you describe what happens in these magnetic vortexes?

MAGNETIC, ELECTRICAL, AND GRAVITATIONAL FORCES ALL IN FLUX.

The magnetic vortexes are definitely something to be avoided. As you will see, this phenomena occurs in different areas on our planet.

ALASKAN TRIANGLE

Another, lesser known, vortex occurs off the coast of Alaska. While Alaska features a harsh environment, including over 100 volcanoes, a huge number of earthquakes, and some of the worst weather on the continent, it also has the highest percentage of people that disappear without a trace, four persons in 1,000. An impressive list of famous people have died mysteriously in Alaska including: Wiley Post, Will Rogers, Ted Stevens, Nick Begich, and Hale Boggs. All of these individuals perished in airplane-related incidents.

In 1972, two famous members of the US Congress, along with another passenger and the pilot, disappeared on a flight from Anchorage to Juneau. Speaker of the House Hale Boggs and Representative Nick Begich were flying in a Cesssna 310 to attend a fundraiser when the plane mysteriously disappeared shortly after takeoff. There was no communication from the aircraft. In spite of a huge search effort that included twelve Coast Guard ships, 400 aircraft, and dozens of other boats, no trace of the plane or the bodies were ever found. While this is the most famous disappearance in this area, it is only one of many.

DRAGON'S TRIANGLE

While the Bermuda Triangle gets most of the publicity, there is an area in the Pacific Ocean that also gets a lot of attention. Another such intersection area lies south of Japan. This area is known as the Sea of the Devil or the Dragon's Triangle. Coincidentally, it is also the location of much underwater volcanic activity. Just like the Bermuda Triangle, there have been many mysterious happenings in the area, including ghost ships, mysterious disappearances of vessels with no trace, and even some lapses in time by aircraft flying through this location. When I asked my spirit guide if there was a dangerous vortex near Japan, he replied:

SMALLER.

Judging from what I read about the area, it seemed to be more dangerous than the Bermuda Triangle. When I asked the question, his answer was:

IN SOME LUNAR CYCLES.

This was the first time I heard that activity in the vortexes was affected by lunar cycles.

SINKING OF THE KAIYO MARU

Perhaps the most extraordinary happening to occur in this vortex was the disappearance of the Japanese sea research vessel *Kaiyo Maru No. 5,* which vanished on September 24, 1952, with thirty-one scientists and sailors on

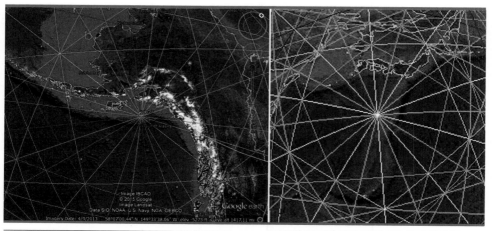

Ley line intersections at the Alaskan Triangle.
Courtesy Google Earth & B. Hagens UVG grid.

Ley line intersections at the Dragons Triangle.
Courtesy Google Earth & B. Hagens UVG grid.

board. Although there was no radio communication at the time of the incident, a massive search did locate some of the wreckage from the vessel. The current theory is that the ship was destroyed by an underwater volcano, but such natural occurrences are indicative of phenomena taking place at the intersection of multiple ley lines. When I asked Mou what happened to the research vessel, he gave me a very simple answer.

IT SUNK.

At least we can all agree on that. My follow-up question was what happened to the vessel.

COMBINATION OF THINGS.

I could tell he was going to make me work for the answers on this subject. What kind of things?

VORTEX.

There are different types of vortexes. When I asked if it was a magnetic vortex, the reply was:

FLUCTUATIONS.

The Japanese government blamed the sinking on underwater volcanic activity in the part of the ocean being investigated by scientists. I asked if the volcanic activity played any role in the sinking of the ship.

ALSO PART.

It also appears that in many instances these locations are affected by volcanic activity as well as earthquakes.

PREDICTING VORTEX ACTIVITY

I asked if there was a time that we should avoid being near one of the vortexes. His answer was:

YES.

I inquired what happened when one of these disturbances took place; the answer was:

MAGNETIC, ELECTRICAL, AND GRAVITATIONAL FORCES ALL IN FLUX.

I was curious what would make Mother Earth exert all this energy along the ley lines that would cause all the activity at the vortexes. He replied:

PLANETARY INFLUENCES.

Needing a little more detail, I asked what caused the forces to increase in the vortexes.

CORE TEMPERATURE IN RELATION TO PLANETARY ALIGNMENT.

I was starting to understand why the aliens considered us inferior beings. There was no way I was going to get my head around what he was trying to explain. At times like this, I find changing the subject is quite prudent. My next question was if there was any way to predict the increases in vortex activity.

TOO MANY VARIABLES. ACTIVITY WAXES ON A 60-YEAR CYCLE.

We were finally getting to something I could understand. So you are saying that activity increases and decreases on a regular basis.

YES.

Where are we in the current cycle?

NEW INFLUENCES IN TEMPERATURE ARE CHANGING THINGS.

Is the current global warming trend natural or manmade?

GREATLY INFLUENCED BY EMISSIONS.

In what way?

MUCH FASTER.

When I inquired if we were near a peak in one of the sixty-year cycles, Mou replied:

1 OR 3 YEARS.

In an attempt to clarify what he was telling us, I asked what year we would see a maximum activity in the vortexes.

2017.

TO SUM IT UP

From our conversations with the spirit guides, we have learned that the Devil's, or energy, vortexes are a very real threat to those caught within the magnetic, electrical, and gravitational forces that are released during such surges. The ancients knew of the proclivity of the earth to exert energies along defined lines and built massive structures, such as the pyramids, to take advantage of the natural energies. It would behoove our modern generations to pay attention to the knowledge of early man. ∞

CUSTER SPEAKS

When the early explorers came to the New World, they claimed all the land for their respective monarchs. Unfortunately, this concept of ownership neglected the fact that there were many Native American communities that had existed and thrived on the land for many generations. As the white man moved westward to "Manifest Destiny," the rights of the American Indian were trampled in the stampede. The Caucasian invaders looked at the Native Americans as standing in the way of progress. As the Indians would find out, there were just too many white men. While settlers rushed westward, the cultures of the white man and the Indians who roamed the plains culminated in the Great Indian Wars of 1876.

MANIFEST DESTINY AT THE EXPENSE
OF NATIVE AMERICANS

Abuse of the Native Americans has taken place since Columbus set foot in America. The United States passed a law called the Indian Removal Act of 1830 that allowed the relocation of the Cherokee, Muscogee, Seminole, Chickasaw, and Choctaw nations to "Indian territory" west of the Mississippi. Referred to as the "Trail of Tears," almost 17,000 members of the tribes were forced to march through winter weather with as many as 6,000 of the participants dying. Forced relocation or moving the Indians on to reservations became the official policy of Washington. By 1837, as many as 46,000 members of the southeastern states' tribes were removed from the tribal homes. The forced expulsion opened up over 25 million acres for white settlement. A lot of land, but not enough to quench the unquenchable appetite of the white man for more property.

By 1876, the Plains Indians were scrambling to protect their way of life. The homestead act of 1860 had resulted in over 600,000 families receiving 160-acre homesteads. Buffalo, the mainstay for the Native Americans, were rapidly disappearing due to heavy hunting by the white man.

As the western migration grew exponentially after the Civil War, the Lakota clung to an area in South Dakota known as the Black Hills. The area had great spiritual significance in their culture and provided bountiful game in the wooded hills. So great was the significance of the area that the US

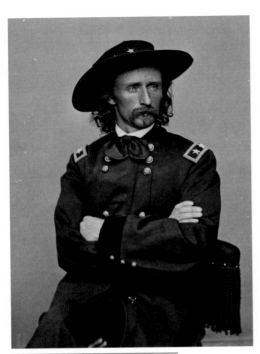

General George Armstrong Custer, commander of the US 7th Cavalry. Photo shows him as General.
Courtesy US Archives.

government signed the Fort Laramie Treaty of 1868 exempting the Black Hills from all white settlement, forever. Unfortunately for the Lakota, "forever" turned out to be six years when, in 1874, George Custer led the Black Hills Expedition and word got out there was gold in the Black Hills.

Custer's path to the Little Big Horn can be traced back to this event, which is when he and the 7th Cavalry led an excursion into the sacred lands of the Sioux Indians to investigate the area's potential for mining for gold. Prior to this time, the Sioux were promised that their sacred Black Hills was protected by treaty. When the news was sent back east of the discovery of gold, prospectors swarmed the Black Hills, driving the Indians from their ancestral ground. While on the expedition, Custer smoked the pipe of peace with the Sioux elders and swore not to wage war. The Indians took the general at his word and did not believe he would participate in attacking their nation.

GOLD ON SACRED INDIAN LAND

The swarm of prospectors and settlers into the Black Hills infuriated the Sioux, and the final blow came when the US government attempted to move them onto reservations. As a result, the Lakota were re-assigned to other reservations in western South Dakota. This action was the proverbial straw that broke the back of the Plains Indians. By 1876, many of the Native Americans had fled the reservations and were gathering in vast expanses of Montana, and the Great Indian War of 1876 began. In one of the largest Indian encampments in history, the Lakota, Northern Cheyenne, and Arapaho tribes congregated in the valley of the Little Bighorn River in an area known as the greasy grass. George Armstrong Custer, the famous cavalry officer who had sworn not to fight the Sioux nation, was about to get the fight of his life.

Throughout American history, few characters have captured the imagination like George Armstrong Custer. From graduating last in his class at West Point and earning fame in the Civil War, to his death in the defeat of the 7th Cavalry at the Little Big Horn, Custer's image is larger than life. Barbara Lee and I were honored to speak with his spirit where he disclosed the true happenings at the battle that ended his life, as well as other events in his career. Many books have been written about the battle, but none have been based on an interview with the spirit of the general himself.

One striking detail as you read the various accounts of the battle is how much they vary in the stated, so-called facts. Early accounts of the battle pictured Custer heroically firing at braves circling the small group of defenders on horseback. This image is what generated the phrase "Custer's Last Stand." Some say the battle lasted for hours, and some accounts say it was over in twenty minutes. Since there were no survivors from the general's battalion, there was no one to dispute the Indians' stories about the battle. Native American survivors were afraid to tell their stories until long after the fighting for fear of reprisal.

When we contacted the spirit of the general, he answered the questions concisely and accurately. As you will see, his spirit displayed the same strong personality traits he displayed in life. During the Civil War, he was promoted to the temporary rank of major general, but at the time of the Indian Wars he held the rank of lieutenant colonel. Throughout this chapter, and in his interview, I will refer to him as general out of respect of his accomplishments.

Anyone who works with the spirit world will realize that they are drawn to people or places. I had been emotionally pulled to the Battle of the Little Bighorn in the summer of 2012 and visited the site with my family. While there, several instances took place that reaffirmed the fact I was led to the place. I met an individual who gave me an introduction to the head of the Crow tribal council that controls the site and, when in a bookstore, I was led to several books giving the history of the battle from the Native American view. After that first visit I could hardly wait to get back to Pennsylvania so we could attempt to contact General Custer, the one individual who could answer my questions concerning the mysteries of the Battle.

THE ARRIVAL OF THE SPIRIT OF GENERAL CUSTER

In late August of that year we attempted to reach the spirit of the general using the channeling board. On that evening we had a general guide named Ramy. I started off by asking if we could speak to the spirit of George Armstrong Custer. Our guide replied:

ASKING FOR A SECOND. I AM NEW AT THIS, SORRY.

When we request a spirit presence, the guide usually asks for a few minutes to find the spirit. I don't know if there is a paging system in Heaven, but somehow they are capable of locating the requested soul. After about a minute, the pointer spelled out:

Who wishes to speak to the general?

I answered that I would like to speak to the general. I could tell the Civil War hero was unimpressed with us by the content of his answer:

Who inquires?

Trying to do some quick explaining, I stated that I was interested in writing a book about the Battle of the Little Bighorn and wanted some firsthand information. My guess is he was still underwhelmed by the next reply:

A book?

Our interview was not exactly getting off to a good start! I told him that I had published a short history on the Battle of Gettysburg and had written about his role in fighting Jeb Stuart on East Cavalry Field. From his next question, I think he was still a bit suspicious.

Are you a Yankee?

Sensing that I could still screw up the interview, I quickly answered "yes." I pointed out that I wrote about his bravery in the fighting, to which he plainly replied:

I was brave.

I could see that a little flattery would grease the wheels of information. In the same vein, I stated that my book pointed out that he had two horses shot out from under him during the fighting at Gettysburg. His reply left no doubt we were indeed having a conversation with the general:

Who is counting?

According to the research I had conducted, the answers reflected his personality in life. Next, I inquired if he would answer my questions about the Battle of the Little Bighorn.

I will answer as I can.

We were about to embark on an informative and important interview. Some historic background is once again required to understand the interview but I will attempt to not make the historic background more detailed or complicated than necessary.

THE SON OF THE MORNING STAR

After earning fame during the Civil War, the general turned to fighting Indians to protect the settlers in the West. In November 1868, the 7th Cavalry under the command of Lieutenant Colonel Custer fought the battle of Washita River in which fifty-three Cheyenne women and children were captured. Among the women was Mo-nah-se-tah, the daughter of Cheyenne chief Little Rock, who was killed in the battle. Custer had a sexual relationship with the Sioux woman, and, in 1869, she bore him a child who was named Yellow Bird. I imagine his blond hair really stuck out in a family of Native Americans! Both were present, unknown to Custer, in the Indian village attacked by the 7th Cavalry at the Little Big Horn.

During the interview with the general, I asked him if he was the father of a child by a Cheyenne woman. He answered the question:

YES, I WAS.

I asked if the name of the child was Yellow Bird and he replied:

YES.

Next, I inquired if he knew his son was present in the village when he ordered the attack and the answer was:

NO.

Barbara Lee asked if he had any regret over being unfaithful to Libby, his wife. He replied:

YES, I DO.

His candid answers verified the historical facts of his sexual adventures.

THE INVINCIBLE 7TH CAVALRY

At the time of the Sioux Indian war, the 7th Cavalry, a force of 700 men, was thought to be invincible. They were armed with the 1873 trap-door carbine, a breach-loading weapon in .45–.70 caliber capable of firing ten rounds per minute, thought to be the most efficient rifle for use by the cavalry. It was quite accurate out 300 yards and proven reliable in combat conditions. Unfortunately, the firearm was very difficult to load while on horseback since it took two hands to open the action and load the cartridge. It was envisioned that the trooper would dismount and use the weapon as an infantryman. Tactics of the day stipulated that the troopers would fight in groups of four, with the fourth soldier holding the horses as the remaining three fired their weapons.

As a sidearm, the troopers carried a Colt Single Action Army revolver that fired six .45 caliber metallic cartridges. Effective range of this weapon fell off drastically over fifty yards. The revolver was used to fight from horseback. The Colt revolver was an effective short-range weapon but difficult to reload from horseback. Much of the early fighting took place with the Indians chasing the Calvary on horseback. They were also issued the standard cavalry sabre, which Custer ordered to be left back to save weight.

In addition, the artillery unit of the 7th had access to two Gatling guns, the forerunner to the modern machine gun, capable of firing 200 rounds per minute. They were mounted on artillery-type carriages and were drawn by horses, similar to standard artillery. The 7th was regarded as superbly armed and the finest fighting unit available to drive the Indians into submission. Custer made the decision that the Gatling guns be left behind because they would slow down the movement of the Cavalry.

THE ARMY CAMPAIGN OF 1876

By the late spring of 1876, the tribes were upset over the living conditions and lack of supplies on the Reservations and began to leave in order to hunt for food. President Grant and the army decided to launch a large campaign to drive the Indians back to their reservations. The generals decided the action would be a three-prong attack that would bring final resolution to the pesky problem of the Native Americans wanting to remain on their ancestral lands. A Dakota column, under the command of General Terry, consisting of about 570 men, would march from Fort Abraham Lincoln, near what is now Mandan, North Dakota. Included in this force were all twelve companies of the 7th Cavalry under George Custer. At the time of the expedition, Custer was to be under the direct command of General Terry.

A second column, commanded by Colonel John Gibbon, departed from Fort Ellis, near what is now Bozeman, Montana. This unit consisted of approximately 400 infantry and cavalry. A third column consisting of 1,300 men, under the command of General Crook, marched from Fort Fetterman in the Dakota Territory. The fort was located eleven miles northwest of what is now Douglas, Wyoming. The battle plan called for the three forces to meet up in the Little Big Horn Valley, the hunting ground of the Lakota Sioux, to engage, and to defeat, the Native Americans in battle, forcing them back to their reservations for a final time. The Cheyenne, Arapaho, and Sioux had a far different idea as to the outcome of events.

CRAZY HORSE DRAWS FIRST BLOOD

On June 17, the plan began to fall apart when General Crook's column was struck in a surprise attack on the Rosebud Creek in what is now Big Horn County Montana. The 1,500 mounted warriors under the command of Chief

Crazy Horse caught the soldiers unprepared and dealt the Army a defeat in which Crook had twenty-eight men killed and fifty-six seriously wounded. Crazy Horse only lost thirteen warriors and his braves now realized that the army was not invincible. Crook had to regroup after the battle of the Rosebud and was delayed from bringing his forces to bear at the Little Big Horn. The other two columns were not aware that General Crook had been delayed and continued with the plan.

In early June, the columns of Gibbon and Terry met up near the mouth of the Rosebud River and joined forces completely unaware that General Crook would not be able to participate in the military action as planned. In preparing their plan of action, Terry ordered the 7th Cavalry under Custer to carry out a reconnaissance along the Rosebud River. His orders gave him the prerogative to "depart" from his orders only to perform reconnaissance upon seeing "sufficient reason." This ambiguity would lead to the downfall of the 7th Cavalry as Custer would make the decision to attack without reinforcements.

In addition to the regular army members in the 7th Cavalry, Custer was accompanied by approximately forty Crow, Sioux, Arikara, and half-breed scouts on his journey to the Little Big Horn. By the evening of June 24, the scouts arrived at high ground known as the Crow's nest, approximately fourteen miles east of the Indian encampment at the Little Bighorn River. The scouts reported seeing a huge pony herd and the massive village, but when Custer arrived he could not see any of the indications of the Indian presence. It is reported that one of his scouts, Mitch Bouyer told him, "General, I have been with these Indians for thirty years, and this is the largest village I have ever known of." When he could not convince Custer, the scout gave away all his belongings believing that he would be killed in the upcoming fighting. His belief indeed came true as several days later his mutilated body would be buried on Last Stand Hill. Why Custer did not heed the warnings is one of the mysteries of the battle.

CUSTER SPEAKS OF HIS SCOUTS

Getting back to our interview with the general, I asked if any of his scouts warned him not to attack the village. According to written accounts he truthfully answered:

YES.

Next, I inquired if he remembered who the scout was who warned not to carry out the attack:

CAN'T REMEMBER.

I guess time can cloud one's memory even when on the other side. It seems as though the general did not get along well with his Indian guides. I asked if he trusted any of his scouts. His answer was:

Not a one.

In retrospect, he should have listened to Mitch Bouyer. When I asked if he felt his scouts sold him out, the answer was:

Yes.

I thought that was a bit of a strange answer, but I guess you have to blame someone. Records show that as many as eight of the Indian scouts died in the fighting. The skull of Mitch Bouyer was found on Last Stand Hill, approximately thirty feet from where Custer's body was found. While the actions of some of the scouts were questionable, many fought bravely to the death. The general either did not believe the reports of his scouts or chose to discount the reports so he could have the glory of defeating the Indians. Custer made the fateful decision to alter his mission from reconnaissance to offensive action and not wait for the reinforcing column of General Gibbon. This decision proved to be the biggest and last mistake of his lifetime.

THE NEED FOR ACTION

During the session, I asked General Custer why he did not wait for the reinforcements under the command of General Terry and Major Gibbon. His reply was:

No time.

His concern over the encampment breaking up and the Indians getting away outweighed the caution of waiting for reinforcements. I asked if was true that Gibbon was three days march away and the answer was:

Yes.

Custer had been pushing his troops to the point of exhaustion by the time he conferred with his scouts at the Crow's Nest, a mountain peak, on the evening of June 24. A distance of about twenty-five miles still separated the troopers from the Indian encampment. His scouts could see the horses of the encampment, but Custer claimed not to see the encampment, even with his field glasses. The general's greatest fear was that the army would be spotted and the Indians would break camp and disappear in the vastness of the plains. Instead of reporting the encampment to General Terry, he ordered his already exhausted men to make an overnight march to get into position to carry out a surprise attack on the Indian encampment.

His initial plan was to launch an attack on the Morning of the June 26, giving him a day to get his men, relatively rested from the march, into position. On the morning of the June 25, he divided his twelve companies into three battalions for the upcoming attack. Three companies were placed under the

CROWS NEST

CROWS NEST AS VIEWED FROM THE RENO POSITION

The Crows Nest where the scouts first realize the size of the Indian village.
Courtesy Barry Strohm.

command of Major Marcus Reno and three under the command of Captain Frederick Benteen. Custer maintained command of five companies, and one was left to support the supply wagon train.

On the morning of the June 25, the day Custer planned to rest his troops, the scouts reported that hostiles had crossed the trail of the Cavalry and that the movement of the 7th Cavalry had been discovered. In spite of his men being exhausted, Custer decided to immediately begin the attack, not giving the Native Americans the opportunity to break camp. The irony is the Indians who discovered the tracks of the Cavalry never reported their presence to the encampment. When the attack began, the village was caught by complete surprise.

As a plan of battle, Major Reno would be the first to engage and attack the flank of Indian village. Captain Benteen would take his men to the south of the encampment and cut off their escape route. General Custer would attack the center of the village with his larger force and the enemy would be caught between the three pincers. The plan looked good on paper, but keep in mind Custer did not know he would be drastically outnumbered or that Crazy Horse had drawn first blood against General Crook, and the third column of the United States Army would play no role in the fighting.

VASTLY OUTNUMBERED

Visitors to the Little Bighorn will be surprised at the large size of the real estate over which the battle was fought. It measures almost five miles by two miles in size. When you take into consideration the dust of thousands of horses and the smoke of the weapons, it is not hard to visualize how the "fog of war" made it very hard for participants to understand what was taking place at the time of the battle. Couriers had to carry messages and commands on horseback, so there would be significant delay before orders could be carried out.

The Indian village on the Little Bighorn consisted of 1,200 to 1,700 lodges and 6,000 to 7,000 Native Americans, including men, women, and children. It was also estimated that one third would be of fighting age or that the 7th Cavalry faced as many as 2,500 able-bodied braves with the ability to fire a weapon. When Custer split his forces between himself, Benteen, and Reno, he had 210 men under his personal command. He could have been outnumbered by as much as ten to one by the end of the fighting.

RENO BEGINS THE BATTLE

About 3:00 on the afternoon of June 25, Custer ordered Major Reno to attack the eastern flank of the village. Without any reconnaissance, Reno's battalion crossed the Little Bighorn Creek and began their charge across open fields with the true size of the village still shielded by trees. To their surprise, they were being met by Northern Cheyenne and Lakota Sioux who were definitely not running away. As if the braves knew this was the last stand in defending their way of life, they were mounting an increasingly steep opposition. As an added incentive, the Indians knew they were defending their families.

When Reno finally saw the extent of the encampment, he realized he was heading for a trap, stopped the charge, and formed a skirmish line with his men, using trees in the area to form a defensive position. His men fired into the village, killing women and children indiscriminately. Among the noncombatants killed was the wife and several children of the Hunkpapa Souix, Chief Gall.

Reno's men continued to fire from their position in the woods for approximately twenty minutes as the warriors swarmed from the village to mount a defense. The braves even set fire to the woods in an attempt to drive the troopers from the area. During this phase of the battle one of his most trusted Arikara scouts, Bloody Knife, was killed while sitting on his horse next to the major. The shot to the head of the scout showered Reno with brain matter, and according to reports, completely unnerved the commander. Reno panicked and ordered a retreat to the higher ground across the river. Many of his men never heard the command to retreat.

Being heavily outnumbered and chased by the mounted braves, Reno led his men in a retreat that became a rout, crossing back over the river and creating a defensive position on a hill overlooking the river and the village. Reno would later report that his losses were three officers and twenty-nine soldiers killed and around fifteen men missing in the rapid withdrawal to high ground. He would also report that he expected to be reinforced by Custer in his charge on the village.

Reno's retreat route up the ravine to high ground.
Courtesy Barry Strohm.

During our interview with Custer, I asked him several questions about what commands were given and the character of Major Reno. When I asked him if he had ever told Reno that he would support Reno's attack on the flank of the village the answer was a definitive:

No.

In the aftermath of the battle, Reno testified before Congress. I asked the general if the major lied to Congress and he replied:

CORRECT, RENO WAS A DRUNK.

I followed up by asking if he was drinking at the time of the attack and he said:

YES.

In order to be perfectly clear, I asked if Reno lied to cover his butt, to which the spirit of the General said:

BASICALLY.

It was obvious that Custer and Reno were not getting along well on the other side. At the beginning of the attack, Custer sent a message to Captain Benteen to rejoin the column and join in the attack on the village. Benteen arrived just in time to assist Reno in establishing a defensive position on the bluff overlooking the Little Big Horn. The troopers dug rifle pits and used anything available in holding off the braves now attacking their position. Visitors to the site can still see the remains of the rifle pits. Had Benteen not arrived when he did, Reno and his men would also have suffered the same fate as Custer.

AN "OH, CRAP" MOMENT

While Reno was engaged in his assault on the east flank of the village, Custer and his men were moving into position on the north side of the river with the Indian encampment still hidden from view. There are a series of ravines, or coulees, that run from the higher ground toward the river. One such ravine is the Medicine Tail Coulee. As Custer and his men topped the hill at the head of the Medicine Tail Coulee, he supposedly saw the size of the Indian encampment

Head of Medicine Tail Coulee where Custer first saw Indian encampment.
Courtesy Barry Strohm.

INDIAN VILLAGE

MEDICINE TAIL COULEE

CUSTER VIEWS VILLAGE FOR FIRST TIME

for the first time. One of the mysteries of the battle is when Custer actually realized the overwhelming size of the opposing force. I asked the spirit of the general when he first learned the size of the encampment. He answered:

WHEN COMING UP ON THE CREST.

Just to make sure there was no misunderstanding, I asked if it was the Medicine Tail Coulee and he replied:

YES.

Since Reno and his men were engaged at that time, the general must have realized that he would have to attack the village if there was to be any hope for success.

CUSTER ATTACKS THE VILLAGE

At the time Custer first viewed the village, it was basically unprotected. The braves had rushed to protect the eastern flank of the encampment from Reno's assault and were busy driving him across the river in his retreat. At the time he topped the ridge of the Medicine Tail Coulee, the Indians were unaware of the threat from the north to their encampment. Custer immediately decided to attack the village by a long charge down the coulee, fording the creek and entering the village. When Custer and his men reached the creek, the charge halted and after a few moments began a retreat back to the high ground north of the Little Bighorn. Another of the mysteries of the battle is why the charge was stopped at the ford of the Little Big Horn.

According to the book *Custer's Fall, The Native American Side of the Story*, written by David Humphreys Miller, only approximately ten armed braves stood between Custer and the village. One of the defenders was a brave named White Cow Bull. Their hope was to hold off the 200-plus charging soldiers until more braves could come to their aid. Years after the battle, White Cow Bull told of firing his musket and hitting a soldier dressed in white buckskins and knocking him from his horse into the river.

THE TURNING POINT

The charge stopped abruptly as other soldiers rushed to keep the wounded man from going under the water. He was loaded back on his horse and the cavalry slowly retreated back up the coulee as a rapidly growing number of mounted braves pursued them. According to the testimony by the Indians involved, a lucky shot from White Cow Bull struck the Son of the Morning Star in the chest and stopped the charge of the 7th Calvary as they attempted to ford the Little Big Horn.

INDIAN DEFENDERS HERE

CUSTER WOUNDED HERE

**Medicine Tail Coulee Ford
where Custer was wounded in the abdomen.**
Courtesy Barry Strohm.

In an attempt to verify what could have been the turning point of the battle, I asked the general if he was shot in his initial attack against the village. His reply was:

WOUNDED. THE SHOT IN TEMPLE FATAL WOUND.

I asked if he knew who fired the shot that wounded him at the creek. His answer was:

I DO NOT KNOW, QUESTIONABLE WHO DID.

I followed up by stating that White Cow Bull claimed that he fired the shot that wounded him at the creek. He stated:

PERHAPS, HE MAY HAVE. NOT CERTAIN WHICH.

AFTERMATH AT LAST STAND HILL

As the battle ended on Last Stand Hill, the squaws came from the camp to make sure there were no survivors. They robbed the bodies of weapons, clothing, and personal effects. Native Americans believed that they would face their enemies on the other side of the life veil. In order to assure victory over their opponents in the afterlife, they would mutilate the bodies of the dead enemy. An enemy with no arms or eyes would be an easy adversary on the other side. When the relief column arrived, the field was covered with mutilated bodies and body parts of the soldiers.

At the time of the battle the braves did not realize they were fighting Custer. He had cut his long blond hair and wore buckskins instead of an officer's uniform. There was one exception to the carnage and mutilation on Last Stand Hill. The body of George Custer was basically untouched. He had a bullet hole to the lower chest and temple as well as a Cheyenne sewing awl in each ear. All his body parts were still connected to his body. Why there was no mutilation remained a mystery.

The most believable story was told to a historian in the 1920s by two elderly Cheyenne women. They were related to Mo-nah-se-tah, the onetime lover of Custer and mother of his child. According to tribal tradition, such a relationship would constitute a marriage. They were also aware that the general had promised not to fight the Indians. The women said they recognized Custer's body and stopped Sioux warriors from mutilating it because he was considered a relative. According to the interview, they inserted sewing awls in his ears so he could "hear better in the afterlife" since he had promised not to fight against the Native Americans.

When I asked the General why the braves didn't mutilate his body after the battle, his answer was different than historical versions. He said:

So I could see all that was around me.

The squaws and braves wanted the soul of the general to understand the extent of his defeat. They felt if they mutilated his body he would not be able to see what was going on around him. Next, I asked if he was conscious during the fighting on Last Stand Hill to which he answered:

Yes.

There are many misconceptions about the final fighting that took place. Early paintings and stories had Custer and his men bravely holding off the Native Americans for a long period of time. In reality, the battle probably lasted for less than thirty minutes as the Indians applied overwhelming firepower and men against the exposed members of the Cavalry. Archeological studies show that many braves were actually armed with repeating rifles. The 7th was outmanned and outgunned.

RENO AND BENTEEN

FIGHT FOR SURVIVAL

As Custer's men were being annihilated, Reno and Benteen were fighting for their lives in a defensive position on the bluffs above the river, about three miles from Last Stand Hill. The Indians had taken the high ground, now referred to as sharpshooters ridge, and were pouring fire upon the soldiers that continued until dark. With the final outcome of the fighting in doubt, the soldiers dug defensive positions with anything available and even killed their own horses to use the corpses as cover.

Chief Sitting Bull of the Hunkpapa Lakota.
Courtesy US Archives.

In reality, the Indians had the ability to overrun the defensive position of Reno and Benteen with their overwhelming number of braves. Chief Sitting Bull argued that if the remaining soldiers were slaughtered, the United States Government would respond with great power and annihilate the tribes. In response to his arguments, the Native Americans broke off the engagement and the remaining troops were saved. I asked Custer if he was aware that Sitting Bull saved the life of Reno and Benteen's men. He replied:

YES.

Next I inquired if he was with Sitting Bull on the other side. He responded:

NO.

When questioned if he ever saw Sitting Bull, his answer was:

YES, GOOD SOUL.

Do you all get along up there?

HA, HA, HA. MORE THAN NOT.

It is nice to know that for the most part, they have made peace and now see each other in that dimension. I can't help but wonder what happens when two spirits don't get along on the other side.

CRAZY HORSE KILLED ME

When I asked if he saw Crazy Horse, his answer caught me off guard.

NO, I STILL BELIEVE HE SHOT ME.

The general believes that Crazy Horse fired the fatal shot to the temple on Last Stand Hill! Chief Crazy Horse never took credit for killing General Custer. Of course he only lived for a little over a year after the battle, and to admit he killed the general would have been a death sentence. When I pointed that out to the general, he replied:

HE DID NOT HAVE THE CHANCE.

In May 1877, after a devastating winter of pursuit, Crazy Horse surrendered to the army at Fort Robinson, Nebraska, in order to protect his people. While Crazy Horse was on the reservation, the army feared he would participate in additional violence, and the warrior chief should be taken into custody. On September 5, 1877, he was killed when a soldier bayonetted him in the back while attempting to arrest the Chief. There are many versions of how the warrior was killed, but from Custer's statement, it seems clear that the spirits think it was a planned murder. I guess they should know.

In the years after the battle, many of the Indians took credit for killing the commander of the 7th Cavalry. Chief Gall of the Hunkpappa Sioux, whose wife and children were killed by the first volleys fired by Major Reno, claimed he had killed the general. When I asked the spirit of Custer about the claims of Chief Gall, he replied:

I KNOW THEY WON. END OF STORY.

I got the distinct impression he was a little touchy about who killed him. Obviously it was time to change the subject. I told him that some historians believe that his plan would have worked if his battalion had continued their attack on the village. He disagreed:

I DO NOT BELIEVE THAT.

So you believe that there was no way you could have won the battle?

CORRECT, I REALIZED TOO LATE. MY BIGGEST ERROR IN LIFE.

I made the statement that no one could have beaten 2,500 braves with his amount of troops. He agreed with me:

TRUE.

After the defeat of Custer and his men, the braves turned their attention on Reno and Benteen's men, entrenched on the bluff approximately three miles from Last Stand Hill. Fighting there continued until darkness and

Last Stand Hill
Site of where Custer was killed.
Courtesy Barry Strohm.

then began with the sun the next morning. Around noon time General Terry arrived with his relief column, and the Indians broke camp and disappeared in the vastness of the plains. They set fire to the prairie grass to cover their trail. There would be no immediate pursuit but time was running out for the plains Native Americans.

NO WOUNDED; ALL ARE DEAD!

General Terry and his men buried the dead in temporary graves and attempted to care for the wounded. Word of the defeat of the 7th Cavalry was sent back to Washington, putting a damper on the Centennial celebration taking place in Philadelphia. Congress attempted to investigate what happened, but in many instances, the testimony was tilted to preserve the reputations of the participants. Major Reno's testimony in particular appeared to be tainted as he tried to cover his butt.

Captain Benteen had basically taken over the command from Major Reno, the highest ranking officer under Custer, during the defensive fighting on the bluffs. His experience with the killing of his scout Bloody Knife had left the major unnerved and unable to make critical decisions. The major never regained his ability to effectively command during the rest of the fighting. Captain Benteen is credited with establishing an effective defense and saving the surviving soldiers.

When I asked Custer if Benteen told the truth after the battle, he replied:

WHAT HE KNEW OF IT.

The Congressional hearings did little to get to the bottom of what really happened to Custer's command. As we came to the end of the session, I began to inquire into other areas of the general's life. There were many rumors that he would use the publicity from the Indian Wars to run for president. When I asked him the question, he answered:

HELL NO, I WANTED TO RETIRE.

Not much doubt in that answer! I said it was not to happen and he agreed with me:

YES.

In military terms, when compared to a Civil War battle like Gettysburg where the count of soldiers killed, wounded, or captured totaled 52,000, the loss of 268 soldiers seems insignificant. Over 300,000 people a year visit the site to view the remnants of one of the greatest losses suffered by the army in the post-Civil war era. When I asked Custer if he realized how many people visited the battle field, he answered:

DOES NOT MATTER TO ME ANY MORE.

The spirit of the general is trying to put the biggest mistake of his life, which cost the lives of himself, two of his brothers, a nephew, and a brother-in-law, behind him. In total, including the scouts, 268 soldiers were dead and 55 were injured. I guess that is a heavy burden, even on the other side.

CUSTER AND JEB STUART

During the Civil War, Custer had gained fame for his bravery and his ability to provide cavalry victories over the formidable Confederate Cavalry under the command of Jeb Stuart. His first victory over Stuart came at Gettysburg when Custer was only twenty-three years old. Federal Cavalry commanded by Major General Phil Sheridan and General Custer were relentless in hunting down Stuart and eventually killed him in the battle of Yellow Tavern on May 11, 1864. When I asked why he was so relentless in pursuing Stuart, he replied:

IT WAS ALL ABOUT RIVALRY. STUART AND I ARE ON FRIENDLY TERMS HERE.

Once again we saw that rivals in life can be friends on the other side.

The defeat of Custer and the 7th Cavalry at the Little Bighorn assured that the Native American way of life would disappear forever as the United States

Confederate General JEB Stuart.
Courtesy US Archives.

Government moved swiftly to avenge the defeat. The army began a scorched-earth policy that forced Sitting Bull to lead his followers into Canada. He held out for four years, but hunger and desperation drove the great chief and 186 of his family members to return to the United States and surrender.

Crazy Horse continued to fight, but the lack of supplies coupled with the severe winter of 1877 caused his followers to abandon him, and, on May 6, 1877, he was forced to surrender at Fort Robinson, Nebraska. Crazy Horse was killed by Indian officers on September 5, 1877. The events around the death of the great warrior chief remain a mystery.

The events that occurred on that day in 1876 represent a great American tragedy, for both the Native Americans and the citizens of the United States. The effects of the Little Bighorn are still felt today as the original residents of our country suffer economic repression and often second-class status. Perhaps the best way to end the chapter is a quote by Luther Standing Bear.

> *Treaties that have been made are vain attempts to save a little of the fatherland, treaties holy to us by the smoke of the pipe—but nothing is holy to the white man. Little by little, with greed and cruelty unsurpassed by the animal, he has taken all. The loaf is gone and now the white man wants the crumbs.* ∞

AUTHOR NOTE

I would like to give special thanks to Patrick J. Hill and Charles Real Bird of the Crow Indian Nation. They provided me with information concerning the life and culture of the Native Americans and access to restricted areas of the Little Bighorn Battle Field that helped me understand the events concerning this monumental clash of two cultures. Their insight and hospitality were much appreciated.

CLEARING THE NAME

OF KING RICHARD III

One day in March 2013, I received a call from Barbara Lee, the clairvoyant that was working with us in our channeling events. I know from experience that you never have any idea what images or messages are given to her by the spirit world, but, as I was about to find out, she was about to top herself. She said that King Richard III had been appearing to her for the last week, and he was telling her that he wanted to clear his name and find justice. She suggested that we have a channeling session and attempt to communicate with the spirit of the King.

It had recently been on the news that physical remains had been found in England that were thought to be the skeleton of King Richard III. From what little I knew at the time, contractors were attempting to build a parking lot and uncovered evidence of an old church. Further excavation uncovered the skeletal remains. DNA tests were being run to confirm the identity of the body. Beyond that, I knew nothing about the history concerning the king except that Shakespeare had written a very unflattering play about him that I had perused in CliffsNotes in college.

Sessions concerning specific spirit requests are better performed in private, so there is no interference from other souls trying to get their message through. His spirit had been appearing to Barbara Lee at her house, so I suggested that Connie and I go to her home with the channeling board and attempt to make contact with the king. In preparation, I researched the history and prepared a list of questions. In my prayers I asked that we could make contact with the king and help him in his quest for justice concerning his life that had ended suddenly in battle over 500 years ago.

King Richard III.
Courtesy Dollarphotoclub.

THE HISTORY OF KING RICHARD III

I know English history is a bit complicated, but bear with me. It makes the interview with the king much more understandable, and I will try to keep it simple. Richard was born in England, in October 1452. He was the youngest surviving son of Richard Plantagenet, 3rd Duke of York, and his wife, Cecily Neville. Richard spent his childhood at Fotheringhay Castle. He had two younger nephews, Edward and Richard, the sons of King Edward IV. At an early age, his family, the House of York, waged the War of the Roses against the Lancastrians to gain control of the country. When Richard was eight years old he lost his father, uncle, and one of his brothers in their fight for the crown. One of Richard's brothers, Edward, defeated Henry VI and took over the throne, taking the name of Edward IV, in 1461, making young Richard a prince.

As Richard grew older, he fought bravely alongside his brother and gained wealth and stature. As Richard grew in power, his right-hand man was Henry Stafford, the 2nd Duke of Buckingham. The Duke, a descendent of Edward, also had a legitimate, though distant, claim to the throne. In 1473, at the age of nineteen, Richard married seventeen-year-old Anne Neville, and they had a son that died at an early age. In 1483, King Edward IV died, and his oldest son, Richard's nephew, barely twelve years of age, took power as the new King of England. The nephew became King Edward V but was not as yet coroneted. Richard had himself appointed as the young king's lord protector, a ruling that in essence allowed him to assume control of the government.

Now here is where the actual history gets fuzzy, and Richard's reputation begins to undergo character assassination by his peers. As the yet-to-be crowned young King Edward V was traveling to London for his coronation, Richard, accompanied by the Duke of Buckingham, met the twelve-year-old king and escorted him to the Tower of London where he was to be lodged for his own safety in preparation for his coronation. His other nephew was brought to the tower later. Throughout history, not much good happens when you are residing in the Tower of London!

About this time, a campaign involving the English clergy, who were in favor of Richard becoming king, condemned the recently killed Edward IV's marriage to Elizabeth Woodville as invalid and their children as illegitimate. An assembly of lords and commoners concurred, making the yet-to-be crowned Edward V, nephew of Richard, ineligible to be the king of England. The assembly petitioned Richard to become king. He accepted and Richard III was crowned in July of 1483. The twelve-year-old Prince Edward was at the time residing in the Tower of London, waiting for a coronation that would never happen.

Within a month of Richard being proclaimed king, the two princes residing in the Tower of London had disappeared and were never seen alive again. There were unsubstantiated rumors that they escaped, but Richard was blamed for their deaths in what was seen as an attempt to remove any threat to his position as king. William Shakespeare wrote a famous play 100 years later in which

Richard III was portrayed as an evil, hunchbacked despot and murderer of his nephews. This characterization stuck through the ages.

By late 1483, a group of gentry that supported the young prince Edward V, who was thought to still be in the Tower of London, plotted a rebellion to overthrow the newly crowned King Richard. The conspirators were joined by the Duke of Buckingham, King Richard III's former right-hand man. When Buckingham presented a rumor to the conspirators that Prince Edward was dead, they devised a plan to bring Henry Tudor back from exile in France. King Richard learned of the rebellion and quickly ended it by force. The Duke of Buckingham was captured, tried for treason, and eventually lost his head. Unfortunately for Richard, the rebellion eroded his support among some very important nobility that held Buckingham in high regard.

By August 1485, Henry Tudor, while living in France, raised an army large enough to challenge King Richard III for the crown of England. The two armies met on Bosworth Field in Leicestershire with Richard commanding an army of superior numbers. What King Richard failed to realize was that a large part of his army had actually turned against him in favor of Henry Tudor. The betrayal by his trusted officers was his death warrant. When Richard realized that his army would not fight, he charged across the field in an attempt to kill Henry Tudor and died in the attempt. His body was buried in a simple grave with its location lost through the ages.

King Richard III is killed on Bosworth Field.
Courtesy Dollarphotoclub.

Henry the Tudor King.
Courtesy Dollarphotoclub.

Once the Tudors ascended to the throne, they attempted to rewrite history. What has become known as the "Tudor myth" represents the fifteenth century, the time of King Richard III and the War of the Roses, a period of bloodshed, treachery, and anarchy. The reign of the Tudors during the sixteenth century is depicted as a time of peace, prosperity, and order.

Historian Thomas More and William Shakespeare, strong supporters of the Tudors, in their writings depicted King Richard III as the worst of despots. In Shakespeare's famous play, the king is depicted as a hunchback that gains the throne by murdering his immediate family: two young nephews, his older brother, and wife. He meets his end when killed in battle by the young and handsome Tudor King, Henry VII. This image has stuck throughout history for King Richard III. He was said to be a tall handsome man of slight build but suffered from a curvature of the spine. His official portraits hide his physical problem but indicate part of his torso had a problem. In life he apparently wore clothes that disguised his deformity.

In September 2012, a team of archaeologists from Leichester University discovered the skeletal remains of a body with a spinal curvature that proved by DNA testing to be the body of King Richard III. What in recent times had been a parking lot proved to be the former site of Gray Friars Church where the body of the fallen king reportedly had been buried. The church was destroyed in the 1530s and its location lost through time. His body will now finally receive the burial fitting for a king of England.

So much for the history lesson. One evening we held a channeling session in an attempt to discover what the former king of England has to say to us.

THE KING APPEARS IN PENNSYLVANIA

I started the channeling session by asking for a master guide. Almost immediately, we received the message:

EPHANEAS, I AM HERE FOR A SPECIAL PURPOSE.

When I inquired as to the special purpose, his answer was:

To help deliver a message as was requested.

My next question was "who requested the message"? His reply was:

Yourself.

It had slipped my mind that I was praying for the spiritual presence of King Richard as well as a few other things. As we had learned on prior occasions, the guides hear the exact words of your prayers and requests. I had been asking for several things, one of which was to better deliver the messages of the guides. When I asked if it was this request his answer was:

Nay.

Not sure what he was getting at, I asked which request he was referring to. His reply was:

Is of God, pray unto thee.

Are you here to answer my requests? He answered:

I can do that albeit we have another waiting.

Starting to realize what was happening since the answers were coming in Old English, I inquired if the person waiting was King Richard. His next response was:

Aye, so pray yea.

Not only were my prayers being answered by the guide, they were being answered in Old English, the actual vernacular of the time of King Richard! My next question asked if King Richard had a message for us. His message was:

I pray your kindness to hear.

Barbara Lee interjected that she had seen the spirit of the king on several occasions to which the guide answered:

Aye, you saw his soul.

TRUST BUT VERIFY

Keep in mind that a heavenly guide passes on the messages of earth-bound spirits on the channeling board. This was an answer from the guide, passing on the message of the spirit. We have been told by the guides to always question the identity of a spirit. As we were told, there are scammers on both sides. I next asked how we could really know that we were communicating with the actual spirit of King Richard III. The next word spelled out on the board was:

FARTHINGAY.

As you remember from the short history, Farthingay Castle was where King Richard grew up. This was definitive proof that we were really communicating with the spirit of the fifteenth-century king of England. Barb then asked if we could speak with him and the answer by the guide was:

AYE, BY THE GRACE OF GOD.

There was no doubt who we could thank for this interview! Whenever we are interviewing famous historical figures, I ask how the spirit prefers to be addressed. When I asked how the spirit of King Richard III wanted to be addressed, he answered:

I AM NOT A KING. I AM RICHARD.

Should we call you Richard? His reply was:

AYE.

I tried to assure him that he was among friends and his message was:

MY BLESSINGS OF GOD ON TO YOU.

My follow up inquired if we were the proper persons to deliver his message, to which he said:

IF YOU BELIEVE I AM OF GOD.

It was becoming obvious that we were dealing with an entity with a deep spiritual faith. I asked if this was the first time he had attempted to make contact with this side of the veil. His answer was:

I HAVE ATTEMPTED THOUGH UPON DEAF EARS.

It must be very frustrating for spirits on the other side to attempt to get messages through to the living when the living do not recognize they are receiving messages.

THE MESSAGE OF KING RICHARD III

We are quite honored, what is your message?

PRAY YOU HEAR ME GOOD. I AM NOT A TRAITOR. I AM NO MURDERER. I CURSE MY KILLERS IN THE NAME OF GOD.

When I asked who his killers were, he answered:

THOSE I LOVED AS BROTHERS. THEY KILLED ME LONG BEFORE I DIED. I PRAY YOU HEAR ME.

We are honored to hear you. His answers were getting emotional:

DEATH TOTALLY RANTS. THEY ARE SCOURGE.

It was becoming more obvious just how strongly the king felt about those who had wronged him. How has your name been tarnished? He answered with one word:

TREACHERY.

Next I asked who was behind the treachery and he replied:

THOSE WHO WERE CLOSE TO ME. MEN I BROKE BREAD WITH.

Keep in mind that his right-hand man, the Duke of Buckingham, led a rebellion to have Richard removed from the throne, and his trusted generals actually turned against him in his final battle. I thought I would forge ahead and ask one of the most debated questions by historians: Had he killed his nephews? He was quick to answer:

I KNEW NOT OF THEIR DEMISE. I SWEAR AN OATH. I LOVED MY BROTHER MORE THAN LIFE. HE WAS A FATHER TO ME.

Barbara Lee then inquired how he came to the throne of England. He replied:

I NEVER INTENDED TO BE A KING. I PREPARED MY NEPHEWS AS ABLE, ALBEIT HE WOULD HEAR NOT.

I attempted to reiterate the question concerning if he knew of the death of his nephews. His lengthy answer made sense:

NAY, NOT SO UNTO ME KNOWN. AS I LEARNED OF THE CONSPIRACY TO RID ME OF MY THRONE, I TOO LEARNED OF THE DEATHS. I FELL TO MY KNEES AND BEGGED MY BROTHER FOR FORGIVENESS AS I HAD FAILED HIM.

I asked: How did you fail your brother?

AS LORD PROTECTOR. I COULD NOT FULFILL MY DUTY.

I then asked how he failed his duty. His answer was:

MY NEPHEW RELEASED ME AS PROTECTOR.

THEY KILLED MY NEPHEWS

This was the first time I heard that the young prince Edward refused the protection of Richard. There is a lot of conjecture concerning who killed the two tower princes. When I asked the direct question he responded with a direct answer:

NEVILLE AND BUCKINGHAM.

The Tower of London where the nephews were killed.
Courtesy Dollarphotoclub.

Neville is the family of the mother of King Richard and as mentioned earlier, led a rebellion against the king. Next I asked where the princes were killed and the reply was:

WHITE TOWER IN THEIR SLEEP.

I suspected that Henry Tudor may have had something to do with the death of the princes. After all, the young princes stood in the way of Henry gaining the throne. The spirit of the king answered:

HE WAS INVOLVED, AS WERE OTHERS. LOUIS ASSISTED HENRY TO THE THRONE. THEY RUINED MY NAME. I HAD SO MANY GOOD IDEAS FOR MY PEOPLE.

I think he is referring to Louis XI of France. Henry had been living in France, so it made sense that Louis would assist the Tudor king. I figured it was no coincidence that King Richard was appearing to us a couple of months after his remains were located after 500 years, so I asked if he arranged to have his body found. His answer was:

FOR CENTURIES I HAD SEARCHED FOR THE PROPER PERSON.

The proper person was Philippa Langley, who formed the Richard III Societies' "Looking for Richard Project." Working with the University of Leichester and the Leichester City Council, they located the remains of King

Richard III under what had been a parking lot. I have no doubt that the spirit of the king was directing the search from the other side.

Studies at the University indicated the king suffered from a condition known as adolescent scoliosis. He had developed this condition after the age of ten and it probably brought him back pain. I asked if his deformity of the back caused him pain and the answer was:

YES.

If you look at his personal images you cannot find any trace of his disability. I inquired if he was successful in hiding his physical problem from the public. He replied:

SLIGHT.

Writings of the times indicate that Richard was slight of build but presented a dashing appearance. When I mentioned this to the king his reply was:

IT DID NOT HELP MY FATE.

During the War of the Roses in England there was scheming and backstabbing that would do credit to a modern television thriller. In an effort to defame the king, rumors were circulated that while Richard's wife was dying, he was planning to marry his own niece, the daughter of his brother, Edward IV. I asked the spirit to comment on the situation. His reply was indignant:

MY BROTHER'S DAUGHTER. I TRIED TO PROTEST AS I KNEW OF HER MOTHER'S PLAN WHILE MY BELOVED LAY DYING. THEY ACCUSED ME OF WANTING TO MARRY THE PRINCESS. FOR SHAME. WHEN I LEARNED OF THE DEATH OF MY NEPHEWS I TOOK NEWS IT WAS MY DEATH WARRANT.

Richard was obviously very upset about the spreading of this rumor. It was becoming more obvious that we were dealing with a man of true faith and honor. He had been caught up in the treachery and politics of a very difficult time in England's history. I told him that he was a very good man. His sad response was:

I THANK YEA. I WAS MOST ALONE AT THE END.

We are much honored to have you with us. We will attempt to tell others. His next words were:

AYE, IT GRIEVES ME TO HAVE BEEN BETRAYED. ALL IS WELL HERE. PRAY THAT THIS STORY WILL ERADICATE THE SUFFERER.

When I told him we would attempt to help he was very firm in his answer:

I WILL BE HEARD FROM AGAIN.

Does that mean you will come through for us again?

IF SO ABLE TO DO. I LEAD THE WAY, AND MY FIGHT FOR JUSTICE IS NOT ENDED.

As a final thought I interjected that we are facing a dangerous enemy today with the threat of terrorist attacks. How should the people prepare and fight them? His insightful answer was:

GATHER STRENGTH IN NUMBERS AND CHOOSE ONLY THOSE WHO ARE LOYAL TO GOD BEYOND ALL ELSE. YOU HAVE MY LOYAL WORD TO PROTECT IF ASKED.

I finished the interview with "God bless you King Richard," and his final remark was:

AND THE GOOD LORD GO WITH YOU ALL.

We had been truly blessed to be given the opportunity to help this good man finally find justice.

In a final note, as I have progressed along this path, my own psychic abilities have increased as I am acquiring the ability to see a spirit presence around me. As I finished this chapter I began to feel very emotional to the point that there were tears running down my cheeks for no good reason. Suddenly, I became aware of the presence of the spirit of King Richard standing near me, wearing flowing green robes. In my mind I heard him say:

THANK YOU.

Upon finishing his two-word message, the apparition of the King faded in front of me. I hope publishing this chapter will help him find the peace and justice he deserves. ∞

CHAPTER 7

GOVERNMENT MANIPULATION

OF THE WEATHER; HAARP; AND CHEMTRAILS

Mark Twain said that everyone talks about the weather but nobody does anything about it. Call me naïve, but I never really thought the government would use geoengineering for political goals or population control. As I started to take an active interest in conspiracy theories, my attention turned to the idea that maybe scientists really are doing something about what is happening in our atmosphere. A little research on the Internet indicated that a lot of people agreed with the theory.

The more I researched the subject, the more I discovered there was a very scientific term that described the science of messing with the weather plans designed by Mother Nature: Geoengineering. Much more prevalent than I ever realized, there is large-scale technological manipulation of the earth ecosystems to alter weather patterns. Much of the study is carried out under the pretext of combatting climate change. It has also become a way of waging a silent weather war or even controlling population growth throughout the world.

As I finish this chapter in the spring of 2015, the East Coast of the United States has suffered two years of record cold temperatures and snow fall. The West Coast is suffering a horrific drought and hot temperatures as an unusual high-pressure area raises the water temperatures in the Pacific Ocean from Southern California to Canada. Fires of historic proportions are ravaging the West Coast. During the winter of 2015, extremely cold weather invaded the southern United States affecting crops deep into Florida. During this period I asked a guide if there were going to be any problems with our food supplies. He replied:

> FREEZING IS A PROBLEM. FOR FOOD IS VERY COSTLY. PRICES ARE HIGH, MOSTLY COLD RELATED.

Simultaneous with this drastic weather, the world has been punishing Russia with crippling economic sanctions and low oil prices for its actions in the Ukraine. Oil is the largest cash producer for the former Soviet Union. Is it possible that the drastic cold for the Eastern United States and Europe would drive up the demand for heating oil, artificially raising the price of petroleum on the world markets? Coincidentally, Russia possesses massive HAARP facilities that would be capable of changing the direction of the upper atmosphere jet stream, directing arctic air or unusually hot temperatures to the lower forty-eight states.

Weather manipulation can be a weapon of ecoterrorism. Countries such as China, Iran, or Russia could simply create freezing temperatures or droughts to have a major effect on our economy. Geoengineering, or manipulation of natural weather patterns, can truly be a clear and present danger.

As I investigated the governmental manipulation of the weather, we questioned the master guides on multiple subjects. From the information given to us, it became apparent that anyone under the age of sixty may have never experienced natural weather patterns. That may seem very hard to believe but as you read this chapter, I think you will be amazed at the amount of government manipulation of the weather that affects all our lives. Your first emotion will be disbelief, but if you only believe a small percentage of the information is accurate, you will still find this chapter quite discomforting.

NOT *IF*, BUT *HOW*

WE MANIPULATE THE WEATHER

During a session in 2013, we were discussing a list of possible conspiracies with a master guide in preparation for this book. I asked if our government could control the weather and his answer was:

YES IT CAN.

Mark Twain must be turning in his grave! In my preliminary research, I had read about a facility in Gacona, Alaska, called High Frequency Active Auroral Research Program, or HAARP. It consisted of a large field of antennas designed to transmit large amounts of energy into the ionosphere, forty miles above the earth. The antennas act as a reversal of what you would expect. They send out high-frequency radio waves instead of receiving them. The project was initiated in 1993 and, by 2008, had expended around 250 million dollars in taxpayer-funded construction and operating costs. This was not a small operation!

According to the official statements in the now-defunct HAARP website, the government described their activities as follows:

> HAARP is a scientific endeavor aimed at studying the properties and behavior of the ionosphere, with particular emphasis on being able to understand and use it to enhance communications and surveillance systems for both civilian and defense purposes.

If that explanation does not give you a warm and fuzzy feeling about the project, here is another interpretation taken from the book, *Angels Don't Play this HAARP* by Dr. Nick Begich:

> HAARP will zap the upper atmosphere with a focused and steerable electromagnetic beam. It is an advanced model of an "ionospheric heater." The ionosphere is the electrically-charged sphere surrounding Earth's upper atmosphere. It ranges between forty to sixty miles above the surface of the Earth. HAARP is the test run for a super-powerful radio wave-beaming technology that lifts areas of the ionosphere by focusing a beam and heating those areas. Weather modification is possible by altering upper atmosphere wind patterns by constructing one or more plumes of atmospheric particles which will act as a lens or focusing device.

The most important part of the project is referred to as an Ionospheric Research Instrument. It consists of a group of antennas that emit a high-powered high-frequency band of energy that actually heats up part of the Ionosphere. This heating of the upper atmosphere creates wind currents that can actually affect the flow of the jet stream.

During one of our channeling sessions, I asked the guide if the government used this facility to influence the weather and once again the answer was:

Yes.

Another inquiry was whether the government influences the weather for political gain and the guide said:

HAARP facility at Gacona, Alaska.
Courtesy www.usahitman.com.

Yes. We know that your government has been doing this especially during the Vietnam conflict in war.

Next I asked if they could create hurricanes and the reply was:

Yes.

When asked if HAARP was used to develop electromagnetic weapons, the guide not only answered my question but delivered a real information bomb:

No. Hurricane Sandy was man made.

Now that I really have your attention, let me do a little historical research so you can understand the full impact of this chapter.

If you believe our government has not participated in weather modification or geoengineering programs, you need only to go online and read a document entitled "A Recommended National Program in Weather Modification," which was prepared in 1966. It was prepared by the National Aeronautics and Space Administration (NASA) for the president of the United States. I have included a photograph of the document that was obtained under the freedom of information act. The guide had already told us that the government was very active in manipulating the weather during the Vietnam War, and this document was prepared in 1966. When spirits speak, I try to pay attention.

PROOF OF WEATHER MANIPULATION

Established in 1993, the HAARP project has generated a lot of controversy over its alleged ability to control weather patterns and possibly a lot more.

A Recommended National Program in Weather Modification.
Courtesy www.geoengineeringwatch.org.

Their website acknowledged that the antennas are used as fire-directed, pulsed-energy beams that can "temporarily excite a limited area of the ionosphere." The ionosphere is an upper layer of the earth's atmosphere that ranges from roughly 30 miles to 600 miles into space and not only protects the earth from space radiation but has a critical effect on the weather. Dr. Bernard Eastlund is the scientist that is linked to the founding of the HAARP project. He holds several patents related to the project that might shed some light on the true purpose of the facility. Here is a quote from his patent:

Temperature of the ionosphere has been raised by hundreds of degrees in these experiments.

Weather modification is possible by, for example, altering upper atmosphere wind patterns or solar absorption patterns by constructing one or more plumes of atmospheric particles that will act as a lens or focusing device. Ozone, nitrogen, etc., concentrations in the atmosphere could be artificially increased.

Electromagnetic pulse defenses are also possible. The earth's magnetic field could be decreased or disrupted at appropriate altitudes to modify or eliminate the magnetic field.

When you compare the stated mission of HAARP with the patents filed by Dr. Eastlund, father of the project, there certainly seems to be some conflict. The HAARP program was the subject of a History Channel documentary that can still be viewed online. A portion of this documentary states:

Electromagnetic weapons...pack an invisible wallop hundreds of times more powerful than the electrical current in a lightning bolt. One can blast enemy missiles out of the sky, another could be used to blind soldiers on the battlefield, still another to control an unruly crowd by burning the surface of their skin. If detonated over a large city, an electromagnetic weapon could destroy all electronics in seconds. They all use directed energy to create a powerful electromagnetic pulse.

Directed energy is such a powerful technology it could be used to heat the ionosphere to turn weather into a weapon of war. Imagine using a flood to destroy a city or tornadoes to decimate an approaching army in the desert. If an electromagnetic pulse went off over a city, basically all the electronic things in your home would wink and go out, and they would be permanently destroyed. The military has spent a huge amount of time on weather modification as a concept for battle environments.

Our little experiment in Alaska has also caught the eye of the European Union. In 1999, they passed a resolution calling for more information on the program's health and environmental risks. The resolution stated that the EU "considers HAARP by virtue of its far-reaching impact on the environment to be a global concern and calls for its legal, ecological, and ethical implications to be examined by an international independent body before any further research and testing." It certainly appears that we have had the attention of the world community for a very long time.

NO MORE HAARP,

HA, HA, HA

Our government claims that the HAARP facility was shut down in June of 2013. About that same time, the website was taken down from the Internet. I asked if the program was still in existence:

YES, MINIMAL.

The fact that the HAARP facility in Alaska was dismantled was verified in a Senate hearing when David Walker, the deputy assistant secretary of the air force for science and technology, testified that the 300 million-dollar facility was indeed being dismantled. He testified as follows:

> *Not an area that we have any need for in the future and it would not be a good use of air force research funds to keep HAARP going. We're moving on to other ways of managing the ionosphere, which the HAARP was really designed to do.... To inject energy into the ionosphere to be able to actually control it. But that work has been completed.*

He actually testified before Congress that the air force now has the ability to control the ionosphere! The entire project was protected by a veil of secrecy, so it is impossible to know what is really happening. I asked the spirit guide if the site in Alaska was replaced with another site. His reply confirmed my suspicions that our government was not going to give up such a valuable weapon.

ADDRESSING THAT NOW.

A year later, I asked our guide about the Alaska facility and what our government has been doing to continue the program. He answered:

KIND OF, MOVED IT TO NEVADA.

I thought I would find out if they simply moved the facility or expanded the program. My next question inquired if our government had more than one facility. He replied:

OF COURSE THEY DO, NEVADA, ARKANSAS, WEST VIRGINIA.

That pretty well puts facilities throughout the country! No wonder we are seeing strange weather patterns!

CALIFORNIA DROUGHT

Speaking of strange weather patterns, it is now the summer of 2015 as I write this, and there has been a historic drought taking place in California for several years. The water of the Pacific off the West Coast started warming in the fall of 2013 and early 2014. When I wrote this, the "blob" of warmer water extended from Mexico to Alaska, and was over 1,000 miles off the California coast. It exhibited temperatures about 2 to 7 degrees warmer than normal. It seemed as though there was a persistent ridge of high pressure that was responsible for the area of warmer water. The Pacific coast suffered warmer air blowing in from the ocean while this area persisted. This warmer air produced less precipitation and accentuated the drought. The drought and warmer temperatures contributed to the wild fires.

Since we know that our government can manipulate the ionosphere and, therefore, the weather patterns, I asked our guide if the high-pressure ridge off the California coast was created by our government. He answered:

Yes.

When I asked why they were doing this, I did not anticipate his answer:

Shift the population.

Why would they want to shift the population?

Bring in new people.

Are you talking about Mexicans?

No.

My next question was if they were planning on bringing in other United States citizens. Once again I do not know if he was pulling my leg or not. He replied:

Aliens.

It is not unheard of to have the guides give us information that messes with your mind. Just to be clear, are you telling me they are planning on bringing in extraterrestrials?

Yes, planned.

I was really having problems with these answers. I tried one more time to clarify what he was saying and restated the question: Are you saying that the drought and violent weather currently hitting California are planned by the United States government and aliens?

Yes.

Is it California or the whole West Coast?

Yes, hot, aliens like it hot.

This is one of those times that I have a very difficult time believing what I am told. However, there must be some ulterior motive for what is taking place in California. If, as we have shown, the government is capable of changing weather patterns, why do they not become involved in alleviating the hot and dry pattern that is going to strangle the people of California?

Texas, too.

During the spring and early summer of 2015, the state of Texas experienced historic flooding. Coincidentally, Texas has been a thorn in the side of the federal government. It has attempted to block Mexican immigration and sued over the current federal health program. They have created more new jobs than any other state in the Union while the National economy has floundered. There are a lot of reasons why those in federal power might have it out for the Lone Star State. While the flooding was taking place, I asked the spirit guide if the government was manipulating the weather to cause the flooding in Texas. His reply was:

YES.

When I inquired if HAARP was playing a role in the weather manipulation, he answered:

SOME.

My next question inquired if the flooding was going to keep up for any length of time and thankfully he replied:

NO.

The guide supplied the right information and shortly after the session the weather began to clear and the flood waters subsided. Apparently someone decided to stop messing with Texas.

WWII WEATHER MANIPULATION

Our efforts to control natural phenomena date back as early as WWII when our scientists attempted to create a tsunami bomb as a weapon to attack Japan. The idea was to create a line of simultaneous explosions off shore to create a tidal wave that would strike the target country. In March 2014, the British newspaper *The Telegraph* published an article about the super-secret tests conducted by the United States and New Zealand governments named "Project Seal." According to the article, the project was launched in June 1944 and could have continued as late as the 1950s.

Records in the New Zealand Archives indicate that 3,700 explosions were conducted in a seven-month period off the coast of Auckland and New Caledonia. According to *The Telegraph* article, experts concluded that single explosions were not powerful enough, and a successful tsunami bomb would require about 2 million kilograms of explosives arrayed in a line about five miles from shore. If you search "Project Seal" you can even find pictures of the tests on the Internet. Imagine the effects of a man-made thirty-foot-high tidal wave on coastal cities. As you will see, other countries have also perfected weather manipulation.

In 1997, US Defense Secretary William Cohen discussed the manipulation of weather events in a conference on terrorism. He stated:

> *Others are engaging even in an eco-type of terrorism whereby they can alter the climate, set off earthquakes, volcanoes remotely through the use of electromagnetic waves. So there are plenty of ingenious minds out there*

that are at work finding ways in which they can wreak terror upon other nations. It's real, and that's the reason why we have to intensify our efforts, and that's why this is so important.

NOT JUST THE UNITED STATES

In June 2014, I asked our master guide what other country was pursuing a plan to manipulate the weather. He replied:

CHINA.

When I asked if they have been successful in their experiments, his answer was:

YES.

The obvious next question was if they have done anything to affect the weather in the United States. He replied:

NOT YET, BUT CAN.

It seems as though all the major powers have the ability to wage weather warfare. A year later, in 2015, we had just gone through a very harsh winter on the East Coast. I could not help but think we might be getting some weather help from other countries. My next question addressed if Russia possessed HAARP facilities.

YES.

With Russia's current aggressive behavior, all we need is for them to have the ability to influence our weather. Personally, I would rather have them keep their Siberian weather in Siberia. Next, I asked if they have the ability to use their facility to influence the jet stream.

IT WILL BE THERE IN ABOUT FOUR YEARS. THIS IS WHAT ALL THE FIGHTING OVER LAND IS ABOUT.

With all the turmoil in the Middle East, it crossed my mind that Iran could create a lot of havoc if they had the power of weather manipulation. When I asked if they had such a facility the reply was:

IN THREE YEARS OR LESS. ONE OF OUR FEARS.

Three years from the date I wrote this chapter would be 2018. The thought of Iran with a nuclear weapon and the ability to influence the weather of other countries is quite terrifying. When I asked if any countries are currently waging war against the United States by manipulating the weather, he replied:

NO, WE ARE.

I guess I should have asked who "we" is.

Usually, when he uses the term "we," he is referring to his buddies from around the galaxy. I asked the question anyway and his response was:

ALIEN BEINGS.

Why are alien beings messing with our weather?

GEOENGINEERING.

I was starting to get the feeling that he was being a bit evasive. When I asked him why beings from other worlds were conducting geoengineering experiments on Earth, he ended the conversation with:

LET IT BE.

There are times when I can take a hint!

MAN–MADE TSUNAMIS

I also inquired if we were capable of creating a tsunami. The answer to that question was quite disturbing:

CHINA.

It is quite unnerving to realize that China is capable of creating a tidal wave! I inquired where they had used a tsunami and the answer was:

JAPAN. GOD WILL HAVE THE LAST WORD AND IT WILL RESONATE LIKE THUNDER THROUGH THE SKY.

Japan has been hit with tsunamis in 2011 and 2013. The worst of the incidents occurred on April 10, 2011, when Japan was struck by an earthquake and tsunami that reached a height of 128 feet and traveled in land as much as six miles in Sendai and killed almost 16,000 people. The tsunami shut down

The Tsunami in Japan.
Courtesy Reuters.

the cooling system of the Fukushima Dalichi Nuclear Power Plant and caused a meltdown that created one of the most serious ecological disasters ever recorded. According to our spirit guide, it appears as though China has found a way to wreak destruction on their longtime enemies by using nature's most terrifying natural disasters. It also appears that they have succeeded in upsetting God by posing as Mother Nature.

If the reader still does not believe that weather can be manipulated, here is an article that was published in January 2011 (www.naturalnews.com/030998_ weather_control_Abu_Dhabi.html).

Weather control is no myth: Today in Abu Dhabi, scientists have successfully manipulated entire weather systems, causing up to fifty downpours of rain across the Al Ain region of the desert nation over the last year. It's all being accomplished by a team of scientists working for Sheikh Khalifa bin Zayed Al Nahyan, the president of United Arab Emirates. They have erected entire fields of giant ionizers to generate waves of negative ions, which rise into the lower atmosphere and attract dust particles. The dust particles, in turn, attract condensation from the ambient air, and when enough condensation is achieved, the clouds can't hold the water anymore and a downpour of rain is unleashed. The whole system was devised by a Swiss company named Metro Systems International. This last year saw huge rainstorms over Abu Dhabi during July and August—months that are normally bone dry in the desert.

If you can create thunderstorms in the desert, I am not sure there is any limit to what is possible in manipulation of the weather.

MAN–MADE DISASTER

I would hope by this time you have at least considered that government manipulation is a strong possibility. During the summer of 2012, we were told by the guides that there would be an October surprise that would have an effect on the presidential election. I misinterpreted the message to believe there would be the normal release of information that would defame one of the candidates. I never imagined the October surprise would be Hurricane Sandy!

In October 2013, our guide reiterated the information we had been given earlier when I asked if our government can control the weather.

YES IT CAN.

My next question got directly to the point: Did the government create hurricane Sandy?

YES, OCTOBER SURPRISE.

When we were told earlier, our interpretation was the surprise was going to be some kind of a political event. Apparently it was the creation of a hurricane that caused major damage to the Eastern seaboard. I reiterated the question concerning whether the hurricane was made by our government. His reply was quite disturbing.

WAS SUPPOSED TO STAY OFF SHORE BUT NATURE PLAYED IN.

Are you saying that Hurricane Sandy was created to gain political advantage?

YES, WE KNOW THAT YOUR GOVERNMENT HAS BEEN DOING THIS, ESPECIALLY

DURING THE VIETNAM CONFLICT IN WAR.

Was our current president aware of the program?

YES.

What technology did they use to create Hurricane Sandy?

THE SAME PROGRAM THAT CREATED MONSOONS IN VIETNAM. SEEDING THE CLOUDS.

When I asked if the people would ever find out that Sandy was created by our government, the answer was:

NO.

In my research, I ran across a website that actually tracks HAARP activity in North America, www.haarpstatusnetwork.com. When you go onto this site you will see a map that is color coded for current activity. Red areas indicate significant outbreaks, pink indicates very severe outbreaks, such as tornadoes, and they also have a rarely seen white color. One of those instances was days before the formation of Hurricane Sandy. This was probably just an unfortunate coincidence.

Another quote from the website reads as follows:

There is a mountain of data including already-conducted experiments, satellite imagery, lab tests of snow, observations on the ground, and multiple existing patents, all of which point solidly to the conclusion that cold and snow storms are being engineered with well-established weather modification processes. Heavy tornados recorded in the last couple of years are also affected by the jet streams.

I then asked if they have any other major storms planned. There was no comfort in the answer from the guide:

IF THEY NEED TO CALL UP, THEY CAN DO SO.

The thought that our own government would actually carry out such destruction and loss of life for political purposes is beyond my comprehension. In this instance, I hope the guides gave me some bad information, but I fear we have underestimated the evil in Washington. In an effort to understand just what our government has the ability to accomplish, I started to pose some general questions. Can our government create earthquakes?

THEY HAVE NOT MASTERED THAT YET.

I thought the "yet" was quite ominous. My next question gave little comfort. Are they close?

A FEW SHAKES HERE AND THERE.

A couple of years ago, an earthquake that struck Virginia that damaged the Washington monument and was also felt in Pennsylvania. I inquired if our government had anything to do with the tremors?

No, NATURAL TREMOR.

Do they have the ability to trigger volcanoes?

YES.

Can we create tornadoes?

NOT AS MUCH.

Has our government ever created a tidal wave?

No.

Who controls the geoengineering weapons?

FEDERAL SCIENTISTS.

What is the most deadly weather weapon created by our government?

THERE IS NO DEADLY WEAPON, ONLY THE WAY IT IS USED.

How long has the government had the ability to control the weather?

DECADES.

If you read between the lines and if you believe others are conducting geoengineering tests, there is little doubt that we have been active in this area for years. In the event that our government has the desire to alter weather patterns, it certainly appears that it has the tools to do it. Before I move on, there is one more area to discuss: chemtrails.

CHEMTRAILS: CHEMICAL WARFARE
IN A TOWN NEAR YOU

We are all familiar with the contrails left by jet airplanes. They are actually a type of man-made cirrus cloud that takes place when water vapor from the jet engine exhaust condenses on particles in the atmosphere and freezes making a visible trail. Chemtrails are formed when chemical particles are released into the atmosphere and the water vapor freezes on these chemical particles. The chemicals eventually float to the earth or can affect natural clouds in the atmosphere. In the photo on the next page you can see a methodical pattern that does not seem to be the traces of contrails from commercial jet aircraft.

In June 2014, I asked our guide whether there was a government program to pollute the atmosphere through the use of airplanes creating trails of chemicals

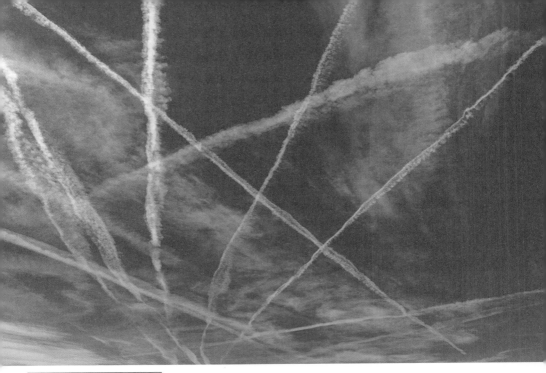

A typical chemtrail pattern.
Courtesy Dollarphotoclub.

in the atmosphere. His answer was a single word:

YES.

When I asked the purpose of the chemtrails, he replied:

DUMP IN THE AIR. SEED THE ATMOSPHERE.

I was curious why the government would want to seed the atmosphere. His answer was really not comforting:

GERM WARFARE.

What is the specific purpose of chemtrails?

DUMP CHEMICALS IN THE AIR TO MAKE US SICK.

Are you saying our government is specifically attempting to make its citizens sick?

YES, POLLUTION, LUNGS.

It seems inconceivable to me that our government would conduct germ warfare against its own people. My next question was why they would take such drastic actions against the population:

Money, modifying population.

Are you trying to tell me that the United States government is attempting to make its own population sick?

Yes.

Still trying to get a grasp on understanding the message, I asked the obvious question: Why are they doing it?

Control.

How do they use it for control?

Disease weakens.

Are you saying they do it only to affect peoples' health in a negative way?

Yes.

If peoples' health is involved, it seemed like one industry would have the most to gain. I asked if the pharmaceutical industry was involved in the funding of chemtrails. His answer opened the door to more questions.

Partially.

In order for such a large operation to take place it seemed obvious that there had to be government involvement. I inquired if there was an individual in our government who was behind the use of chemtrails. He replied:

A group.

Trying to narrow down the identity of the culprit, I asked: Is it a group of individuals within the Pentagon?

Within.

Since this is a conspiracy book, I had to know if our presidents knew of the operation. His response was:

Peripherally.

When I inquired who else was involved, his reply was:

CIA director.

At this point I could not help but remember how our last director of the CIA, General David Petraeus, was forced to resign for having an affair with his biographer. I had always respected the general for his military leadership and it bothered me how he was persecuted for acts that were probably being carried out by more than half the politicians in Washington. When I asked if he was involved with the chemtrails, my suspicions were confirmed.

Did not agree.

Is that one of the reasons he resigned?

YES.

I always believed there was a reason why the general never defended himself publicly. Anyone in his position would be well aware of where all the skeletons were buried. I inquired if he was threatened to keep quiet?

YES. HE AND HIS FAMILY.

When I questioned if he would ever speak out the answer was:

NO.

As I look at the websites talking about chemtrails, it seems like there is an awful lot of it going on today. When I asked if the use of seeding the atmosphere was increasing, the guide replied:

STATIC.

At least the use of poisoning the atmosphere was not growing. When I inquired how long the government was going to continue to sicken the population, his answer was:

DEPENDS ON PROFITS.

Do some of the chemical trails cause cancer?

YES.

What areas of the country are hit the hardest?

THE WEST: TEXAS, MEXICO, CALIFORNIA.

Since my home is in Park City, Utah, I asked if the Salt Lake City area, already known for high-pressure inversions and air pollution, was also affected by the germ warfare. I did not like his answer.

YES, ROCKIES.

Why the Rockies?

BARRIER.

I guess most of the crap dumped on California will drop out over the Rocky Mountains.

Think of the control the government would have if they manipulated our health care system to the extent that individuals could not determine their medical care, and decisions were left up to bureaucrats. Has anyone noticed that this is exactly what has been taking place with the government takeover of our health system? Add to the equation that the government could create disease and sickness that would drive people to the regulated health care system. The whole process creates a draconian conspiracy that could destroy our entire way of life as only a select few are selected for cure from a man-made illness. I asked the guide if there was anything that could be done to stop the conspiracy. His comment was direct and to the point:

IT MUST BE. ALL PART OF THE PLAN TO DESTROY EARTH AS WE KNOW IT.

GLOBAL WARMING

Another area where the US government is forcing change is global warming. I would point out that since the planet seems not to be warming for the past several years, they changed the term to "climate change." When I asked if they were using geoengineering to promote global warming, the answer was:

YES.

Vast fortunes are being made in the name of global warming. I guess it is only common sense to assume that if the government has the tools to manipulate the weather, they will manipulate it to their advantage.

As you can see, our government has been attempting to control various natural occurring phenomenon, such as weather, tsunami, hurricanes, earthquakes, the health of our population, and whatever else they are capable of mastering. In addition, the government, under the control of the CIA and Pentagon, is actively attempting to affect the health of the citizens by spreading pollution and chemicals in the air over the United States through the use of chemtrails.

Our master guide providing much of our information in this chapter was Saint Martin of Tours. One of the best known and recognizable of the Christian Saints, he lived from 315 AD to 386 AD and is known to have created many miracles in his lifetime. Perhaps the way to bring this chapter to an end is to quote a statement by our master guide. At the end of the session I asked St. Martin if he had any other messages. He replied:

IT ANGERS ME AND I SHOULD NOT FEEL ANGER. THANK YOU.

If the actions of our government are enough to anger a Saint in Heaven, retribution from above must not be far away. I hope it comes in time to save us all. ∞

TINSEL TOWN TRAGEDY

In October 2013, I received a phone call from my clairvoyant friend, Barbara Lee. She said that a spirit was making his presence felt and was appearing to her. I know from experience that when a deceased soul wants to get a message to this side of the veil, they often start by contacting Barb. When I inquired who was trying to get a message through, she said it was Robert Walker. My response was "who in the hell is Robert Walker?"

FAMOUS IN THE '40S

Robert Hudson Walker was a movie star in the 1940s. He was married to Jennifer Jones and two other women—seemingly typical of the Hollywood lifestyle. According to newspaper articles, he died in 1951 at the age of thirty-two from an overdose of prescription drugs, the way a lot of stars meet their end. His best role was in Alfred Hitchcocks's *Strangers on a Train,* which hit the theaters in 1951, the year of his death. The actor was apparently in an emotional state created by drinking. The doctor gave the actor a shot of a sedative that interacted with the alcohol in his system and caused Walker to stop breathing. No autopsy was performed, and his death was declared accidental. By the time of his death, Robert Walker had appeared in twenty movies, interacting with many of the best know stars of the time.

Robert Walker and Judy Garland. From the 1945 romantic drama *The Clock*.
Public Domain.

Since this was a special session, we went to Barbara Lee's home so there would be no interruptions. I started by asking for a master guide who would help us reach Robert Hudson Walker. Almost immediately the pointer spelled out the name of our guide:

Roger.

When I asked if he had ever been with us before, his reply was:

Yes.

Spirit guides have different specialties over there. I believe Roger works with deceased souls. Next I inquired if the spirit of Robert Walker was present. The reply was:

Hello, he is here. He is anxious to speak.

I started by asking if he had any messages for Barbara Lee.

Thank you for listening

The spirit had found a willing and sympathetic listener! I started by asking what he had to say to us. He lost no time.

I was murdered. Why did they do this to me?

I followed up by asking what they did to him. His reply was :

I was killed.

That was definitely not the understanding I had from reading the articles concerning his death.

HE TOOK MY WIFE

His previous answer was certainly getting to the point of his visit! I asked why he was murdered.

He took my wife who I dearly loved. Thing is, she says she always loved me, too.

Walker was talking about his wife, Jennifer Jones. She left him for the famous producer David O. Selznick. In 1941, Jennifer Jones began a long-term affair with the famous producer. Under his guidance she was given more and more important roles in his movies. Jones and Walker separated in November 1943 when he learned of the affair. In 1944, while still technically married to Robert Walker, she won the Academy Award for Best Actress for her performance as Bernadette Soubirous in *The Song of Bernadette*. In 1945, she divorced Walker. The bottom line is his wife apparently loved fame more than their personal relationship.

My next question: Are you saying that your wife really loved you in spite of leaving for another? His reply was:

Yes.

I then asked why she left him, and the answer was:

She didn't want to.

Apparently spirits on the other side can have trouble facing reality, even if it happened over sixty years ago. I asked if he ever sees her on the other side. He replied:

We are in contact.

I would think it was hard for the actor to forgive his ex-wife for the decisions she'd made while they were married. Barbara Lee began to feel a constriction in her throat. She has the ability to often feel the pain suffered by the spirits when she is in close contact, like during this session. She asked if he had trouble breathing when he passed. His answer was:

Yes, could not catch breath, thank you.

NOBODY CARED!

I thought I would inquire about the details of his death: What was the situation when you were killed? His answer surprised me:

No one else much cared.

The actor was saying that there was no one close enough to question how he died. I asked if he was talking about the people around him. His answer was:

Yes.

This was obviously before the days of *CSI*, but I asked if the police were involved. His answer revealed the power of the movie producers of the time. It was:

No police. Hushed up.

No wonder there was no autopsy! I asked if he was poisoned. His reply was:

Drugged to death.

My follow up addressed if they gave him narcotics and his answer was:

Yes.

The news reports indicated that he was injected with amobarbital for sedation by the doctor. His death was blamed on an interaction with alcohol. I asked if he was drinking and his answer was:

I was not.

Was it made to look like an overdose? His reply was:

No, it was made to look like an accident.

As the session was progressing, I was becoming aware that my back was beginning to hurt but did not mention it. Barbara Lee suddenly mentioned that her back was beginning to ache. She asked if the spirit had back troubles. He replied:

YES.

When I did additional research, I found out that he had tried to enlist in the army but was turned down because of a bad back. Both of us were now feeling his physical problems.

THE DOCTOR DID IT

I thought I would get to the heart of the matter, so I asked who was responsible for his murder. He replied:

DOCTOR.

Next, I asked who was responsible for hiring the doctor to kill the actor. Not surprisingly, he answered:

I WILL NOT REPEAT HIS NAME.

Are you saying that David Selznick was responsible for your death? His reply was:

THAT IS EXACTLY WHAT I AM SAYING.

There was no doubt in the words of the spirit of Robert Walker who was responsible for his death.

Selznick was married to Jennifer Jones from 1949 to 1965. In 1954, she and Selznick had a daughter together. I asked the spirit why the producer would want to have Walker killed two years after he married the actor's ex-wife. I asked the spirit why the famous producer wanted to kill him. He answered:

PHYLLIS [JENNIFER JONES'S REAL FIRST NAME] WANTED BACK WITH ME. HE DRUGGED HER, TOO.

According to the words of the actor, the director had Robert Wagner killed so Jennifer Jones would remain with him. I asked if she'd considered suicide. He said:

VERY DEPRESSED. NO CHOICE.

Barbara Lee interjected that he must have been a real monster. His reply was a single word.

WICKED.

I stated that she seemed to go along with leaving him. After all, she had a long-term affair with Selznick and divorced Walker. His answer was:

HER INTIMATE FRIENDS KNEW.

Next I asked if she feared the movie mogul. His reply was:

I BELIEVE SHE DID. I WAS THREATENED TO LEAVE HER ALONE. SHE WAS SCARED TO DEATH OF HIM.

He then went on to say:

I KNEW HE HAD IT IN FOR ME.

An indication of the vindictiveness of David Selznick occurred in 1944 during the filming of *Since You Went Away*. Both Jones and Walker had starring roles in the movie, in which they portrayed young lovers. Jones and Walker separated in 1943, during the filming of the movie. After the separation, Selznick insisted that Walker and Jones repeat take after take of the love scenes since they were so troublesome to Walker. No wonder the actor developed emotional and drinking problems!

**Robert Walker and Jennifer Jones.
Scene from *Since You Went Away*.**
Public Domain.

After the breakup of Walker and Jones, the actor began to suffer mental and alcohol addiction symptoms. In 1948, he married the daughter of John Ford, the famous director. Their marriage lasted only five months. After numerous arrests for drunkenness, he was committed to a sanatorium. After his rehabilitation, he went back to acting. In 1951, he was back on top with perhaps his most outstanding role in the Alfred Hitchcock thriller *Strangers on a Train*. By the middle of 1951, he had a major part in the movie *My Son John*, along with Helen Hayes and Van Heflin. On August 28, 1951, his housekeeper reportedly found him in an agitated state and called his psychiatrist, Dr. Frederick Hacker, to calm the actor down. As the story goes, the actor had a rare allergic reaction to the sedative administered by the doctor.

I decided to try to get more facts concerning the night of his overdose/murder. I asked where the murder took place. His answer was:

IN MY HOME.

Next, I inquired what room, and he answered:

BEDROOM.

What was the name of your doctor? His reply was:

HACKER, THERE WAS ANOTHER. I DID NOT KNOW HIM; HE CAME IN AFTER I WAS GONE.

Dr. Frederick Hacker was indeed the one present when Walker passed. Trying to get more details of the incident, I asked if his housekeeper deceived him. He said:

I WAS FOOLED BY HER KINDNESS. I NEEDED THE HELP AND SETTLED.

If the actor had truly been murdered, the housekeeper would have to know what really happened. Here is the obituary from the *New York Times* (August 30, 1951) that gives the official rendition of his death:

Dr. Frederick J. Hacker, a psychiatrist who had been treating Mr. Walker for eighteen months, said he had been called about 6 p.m. by the actor's housekeeper and found him in "a highly emotional state." He kept saying, "I feel terrible, Doc—do something quick," the psychiatrist reported, adding that he did not know whether the actor had been drinking.

A seven-and-one-half grain dose was given, Dr. Hacker said, only a fraction of previous doses the actor had received, but almost immediately he turned blue and gradually stopped breathing—a reaction which, Dr. Silver said, occurred only about once in 10,000 cases. He certified the death as natural, due to respiratory failure.

Dr. Victor Cefalu, assistant county coroner, said today that a fifteen-grain dose could be toxic, and that the drug accumulated in the system.

The coroner's office said there would be no autopsy unless a member of the family requested it.

If you read between the lines of the obituary, you can see that the actor had been accurate in his description of the events surrounding his death. According to the article, the odds were 10,000 to one that a dose the size claimed by Dr. Hacker could have killed Robert Walker, and no autopsy was ordered. In hindsight, it certainly appears that there is much more to the actor's death.

I thought I would inquire about the movie mogul who was behind the death of Robert Walker. My next question asked if Selznick was associated with the mob. Walker replied:

HE HAD CONNECTIONS EVERYWHERE.

KARMA

My next question was if he ever sees the director on the other side. His reply caught me a bit off guard.

I HAVE NOT. HIS DAUGHTER KILLED HERSELF. THAT WAS PAYMENT FOR HIS SINS.

Jennifer Jones and David Selznick had a daughter who was born in 1954 and committed suicide by jumping from the twentieth-floor window of a building in Los Angeles in 1976. Selznick died in 1965, so his spirit was probably forced to watch his daughter kill herself from the other side. It seems as though there are many ways to pay for the sins committed during a lifetime. When I asked if he is paying for his sins, Walker answered:

HE IS NOT HERE THAT I HAVE SEEN.

I inquired if there was a place for those that do evil and the reply was:

YES, I WOULD HOPE FOR IT.

Barbara Lee had mentioned that she was also having visions of Alfred Hitchcock and Peter Lorre. This is going to get a little weird, but every time she sees them, they have a cigarette lighter in their hands. I started this segment of the session by asking if they had anything to do with his murder. Walker's answerer was:

BOTH MEN KNEW HIM WELL AND WHAT HE WAS CAPABLE OF.

Do you talk to them over there? His answer to that was:

YES.

Old friends seem to hang together on the other side. As I mentioned, whenever Barbara would see them, they were holding a lighter. She and I had discussed the meaning of the lighter but had no good idea as to its meaning. I asked Robert Walker the meaning of the symbolism. Once again his answer surprised me. He said:

AT ONE POINT WE ALL WANTED HIM TO BURN IN HELL.

Once again we see that spirits can maintain strong hatred on the other side of the life veil. Next, I asked if all three of them had run-ins with Selznick, to which he replied:

YES.

My next question inquired how Peter Lorre was involved.

BOTH JEWS. LORRIE FLED FROM NAZIS AND HE (SELZNICK) WAS A CLOSET COMMIE.

I tried to clarify his statement by asking if Peter Lorre was a Communist. The reply was:

HE HATED THEM.

Next I asked if David Seltznick was a Communist. He rapidly spelled out:

HE WOULD MAKE YOU THINK NOT, BUT HE WAS.

Will that information ever come out? Walker said:

IT WILL COME OUT, IN A BOOK BEING WRITTEN BY A BIOGRAPHER.

REALLY UPSET

I asked if the book was being written now and he replied:

RESEARCHED. I WILL NEVER SPEAK HIS NAME!

The hatred was so strong for the spirit that he would not even mention the name of person who ruined his life. We had been given a wealth of information about the life and death of the actor. I asked him what he wanted us to do with the information we had gained during the session. He answered:

HARD TO INVESTIGATE NOW AS ALL INVOLVED ARE OVER HERE.

Are you saying everyone involved with your murder is now dead? He replied:

YES, I BUT WANT MY MEMORY CLEARED.

Next, I asked if he thought people had bad memories of him.

THEY DON'T REMEMBER AND WHAT IS WRITTEN LEADS TO A DRUG OVERDOSE.

I commented that after all the time that has passed, I don't see how there can be justice. His reply was:

THERE HAS BEEN ON THIS SIDE.

I asked: Is Selznick paying for his sins? He answered:

HE IS NOT HERE THAT I HAVE SEEN.

I decided to finish the interview with some general questions. I inquired if he and his wife were okay over there and the answer was:

YES.

Troubled souls rarely make the decision to reincarnate and come back for another life experience, but I posed the question anyway. We were not surprised when the answer was:

NO.

My final question was if his children blamed his doctor and he replied:

NO, I THANK YOU FOR YOUR TIME.

A VERY UPSET SPIRIT

Robert Walker had a lot to say and I hoped our session gave him some closure.

Our master guide, Roger, had done a good job of helping the actor get his messages through to us that evening. As we were closing for the evening I asked Roger about the emotional state of the spirit of Robert Walker. The guide replied:

SUBJECT WAS VERY EMOTIONAL AND ANGRY.

I commented that I hoped we could help give him some closure to which the guide replied:

IT IS A GOOD START.

I knew the answer to the next question but I asked it anyway. Is it part of our mission to help troubled souls? He replied with a single word.

YES.

When I asked if he had any other messages Roger replied:

DONE HERE. THANKS BE TO GOD.

I could not have said it better myself. ∞

CHAPTER 9

BIGFOOT

FACT OR FICTION

I never took much stock in the whole Bigfoot thing. One evening in October 2013, I was involved in a channeling session with a master guide named Thomas. My objective on that particular night was gaining information about various subjects to be included in this conspiracy book. As we came to the end of the session, I threw in a question about Bigfoot, almost as an afterthought. When I asked if Bigfoot existed, he answered:

ACTUALLY, YES.

That was not the answer I was expecting! I followed up by inquiring if they existed in the United States and he replied:

SCARCE.

The more I channeled about the existence of Bigfoot, the more bizarre the information given me by the spirit guides became. In 2014, we gained the ability to contact the spirit of an alien. In many sessions he provided information about widely varied subject matter. I had read one theory where the Sasquatch were believed to be aliens, so who better to ask than an alien guide. When I asked Mou about their existence, you will see that he added an entirely new dimension to the story, literally and figuratively.

Up until the first session in 2013, the concept that a huge, ape-like creature could exist in our modern society without being killed or captured seemed inconceivable to me. If you do research on the Internet, you will become immediately aware that there are large groups of people who take their existence very seriously. There are even television shows dedicated to attempting to prove that Bigfoot is very real. Probably the most interesting fact is that, in spite of all the attention and hours of investigations, there has never been definitive proof of their existence.

As you read the literature, and there is very much of it, you will see that sightings are referenced in many parts of the world. Perhaps the earliest reported sightings have taken place in the Himalayas of Nepal where the beings are referred to as Yeti or the Abominable Snowmen. There are even pictures available showing skeletal remains of skulls and hands. If you think Bigfoot is not big business, I just searched it on eBay and there are over 52,000 items listed!

In North America the creatures are referred to as Sasquatch or Bigfoot. If you are from the south, in states such as Florida, they are called Skunk Apes. It is alleged from persons who have observed this warm-weather variety that they have a pungent odor, similar to that of a skunk. I guess we have to assume that they have little time for bathing.

TRACKING BIGFOOT, OR NOT

Adding to the mystery of their presence, there have been many documented incidents of humans impersonating the creature in photographs and creating large footprints that supposedly represent the tracks of Bigfoot. In 1982, Michael Dennett wrote an article for the *Skeptical Inquirer* stating that a logger named Rant Mullins had carved wooden feet and perpetrated a hoax on researchers that dated back to as early as 1930. He was apparently responsible for leaving footprints around the Mt. St. Helens and Northern California area for many years. You can even go online and see a photograph of him holding the carved wooden feet that he used to fool investigators for many years.

SEEING IS BELIEVING, OR NOT

Reported sightings of Bigfoot is not a modern phenomenon. According to the *The Bigfoot Casebook* (Bord, 1982) recorded sightings date back to the 1830s. On one website, www.joshuastevens.net, there is a graphic that shows 3,313 documented sightings from 1921 to 2013. The map is quite interesting with many sightings taking place in the Pacific Northwest, Ohio, and Florida. The state with the fewest sightings appears to be Nevada. My guess is that Sasquatch are anti-gambling. A more realistic theory would be that they do not like desert country because there is little vegetation for their concealment.

Perhaps the most famous motion picture of a Bigfoot was taken on October 1967, by Roger Patterson and his partner, Robert Gimlin. It was supposedly taken on Bluff Creek about twenty-five miles northwest of Orleans, California. Through the years, the image has been proven to be a fake by some authorities and a non-human creature by others. Patterson died of cancer in 1972 and swore the movie was authentic. His partner, Robert Grimlin, denies being involved in any hoax and swears the encounter was real.

One evening we were channeling with our alien spirit and I asked him if the Patterson movie was real. His answer was short and to the point.

No.

Congratulations to the scientists who insisted it was a fake. It is events like this that give Bigfoot hunters a bad name. According to our guides, there is no doubt that if Sasquatch exists, he is one of the most elusive creatures on this planet.

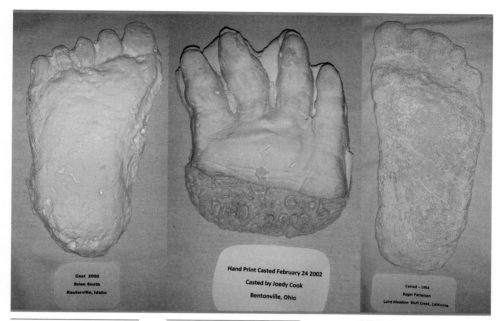

Cast 2000
Brian Smith
Keuterville, Idaho

Hand Print Casted February 24 2002
Casted by Joedy Cook
Bentonville, Ohio

Casted – 1964
Roger Patterson
Laird Meadow Bluff Creek, California

Cast of a bigfoot footprint. Cast in 2000 by Brian Smith, Keuterville, Idaho.
Courtesy Barry Strohm.

Cast of a bigfoot handprint. Cast on February 24, 2002, by Joedy Cook, Bentonville, Ohio.
Courtesy Barry Strohm.

Cast of a bigfoot footprint. Cast in1964 by Roger Patterson, Laird Meadow, Bluff Creek, California.
Courtesy Barry Strohm.

In modern times it is easier to get images of Bigfoot tracks. In the Digital Age, anyone in the world can buy a cast of an alleged Bigfoot print and presumably make tracks that would very closely match tracks accepted by some as authentic. You can even attend conventions around the world with persons dedicated to proving the existence of the allusive creature. I have included some of the casts that are on public display. With all the activity, you would think that someone would have come up with definitive evidence. As you are about to find out, there is reason why they are so elusive.

WHEN IN DOUBT, ASK AN ALIEN

One evening, in the Spring of 2015, I brought the subject up with our alien guide. In my first question I attempted to reiterate what had been told to me a year earlier and inquired if Bigfoot existed. He was quick to answer:

SURE DOES.

I thought I would try to confirm their appearance so I asked him how tall they were.

8 FEET.

When asked how much they weigh, he pretty much confirmed visual estimates.

600 POUNDS.

From all reports, they appear to be some type of an ape/human cross breed—like something that Charles Darwin referred to in his evolution of man theory, except this would be an ape on steroids. I inquired as to the genetic classification of the species.

HE WILL BE CLASSIFIED AS A GREAT APE. EARTH GENES.

My guess was they had to be pretty intelligent to avoid detection all these years. Next, I asked if they were more or less intelligent than humans.

LESS. THEY ARE LIKE WHALES IN MINDS. THEY FEAR MAN.

Judging from the map I referenced earlier, they must be in quite a few places. I asked where most of them live.

THEY ARE EVERYWHERE. YOU JUST HAVE TO KNOW WHAT TO LOOK FOR.

I asked him if there were many of them in existence.

MANY, MANY.

If there were many of them around, how come they are so hard to find? I asked where they live. He replied:

DARK TREES, WHERE IT IS THICK.

That certainly explains why there are not many sightings in desert states. At the time, we were spending most of our time in Pennsylvania. I asked if there were many in that state.

MANY.

The state is definitely large in size with much of it wooded. We were once told that all things have a purpose in God's eyes. I asked what was the purpose served by Bigfoot?

THEY ARE NATURE MADE. THEY ARE A PRE-MAN.

He ducked that question nicely. How long have they been on earth in their present form?

7,000 YEARS OR MORE.

They have been spotted in some of the harshest environments on earth. I asked how they survive?

HUNTING, GATHERING.

If there are so many of them and they occur almost everywhere, they must not only be somewhat intelligent, but they must have some very strong opinions of humans. I asked Mou what they thought of the earthlings who keep chasing them around, and if they meant us any harm.

No, THEY MEAN NO HARM AND THINK YOU ARE AN ODD BEING.

At last we found something I have in common with Bigfoot. I also think there are a lot of odd human beings, especially around Washington, DC.

I had read online that the reason Bigfoot was so elusive was that they were a type of alien. If anyone should know, it would be Mou since he was one. His answers were about to lead us in a very unexpected direction. I started by asking if they were brought here by aliens. His answer was:

No.

So much for that theory!

THE OTHER SIDE OF HERE

When I asked if they were a type of alien, his answer began to get very complicated.

WELL, TWO DIMENSIONAL.

I should have stopped asking questions while I knew what he was talking about! He had talked about multiple dimensions before, but I always though two dimensions was a flat surface. In his world, "two dimensions" has a very different meaning. I tried to understand what he meant and asked where they live. His answer almost made me lose what little hair I have left.

ON THE OTHER SIDE OF HERE. THERE IS A HERE AND THE OTHER SIDE OF HERE. THE OTHER HERE. IT IS LIKE SOUND. THERE IS A C AND NOT A C AND IF YOU PLAY THEM TOGETHER THERE IS A SILENCE.

I told you I should have stopped asking questions while I was ahead. Forging onward, I inquired if he was saying that the dimensions offset each other like sounds offset each other. He agreed with me, I think.

RIGHT, SO IN THE HERE AND NOT HERE THERE IS A DOOR.

This was going from bad to worse. Now he was talking about a door in the not here. I confessed I was having trouble understanding his last answers about the two dimensions and asked: What is the other side of here? I think he started to take pity on my lack of understanding by somewhat agreeing with me that he has some problems understanding the multiple dimension thing.

ME TOO. ANOTHER DIMENSION IS WHERE THE PAST AND THE FUTURE ALL LINE UP WITH THE NOW.

With that answer, my sense of understanding was going from worse to "oh shit." In the back of my mind I remembered Einstein talking about a parallel universe. When I asked if he was referring to a parallel universe he answered:

Somewhat. It is like an opposite to here.

I blurted out, "what is not here?" His answer did not help.

There.

This was starting to sound like an old Abbott and Costello skit. I asked if there was life there and he replied:

Very much.

At least there was life in the "there," wherever "there" is. In what seemed like an obvious question, I asked why they would ever come here.

Food. There is better grass. The grass is always greener. There is sweeter water. There is fatter food.

Let me attempt to recap what I think we were just told. Sasquatch actually live between two different dimensions. When they are in the other dimension they are in a world unseen by humans. Apparently there is better food and water in our dimension, so they come over to our side to hunt and gather food. I asked why they are able to escape detection when they are on our side.

Just learned to hide in the doors.

Now he was telling me that there was some type of door or entrance between the dimensions. I tried to clarify by restating that when they are detected they simply go through a doorway to the other dimension.

They walk through the door. You can see one and they are there. Then they are not.

I cannot imagine that one has never had an accident or died while in our dimension. I asked Mou how come a body of a Sasquatch has never been discovered.

They are drug back.

I guess that makes sense. The others drag the bodies back through the door to the other dimension. My final question was if we would ever discover one.

One time there will be one found.

My guess is that sometime an individual will kill one of these mysterious creatures. I would be willing to bet that when you began to read this chapter you never expected to learn that Bigfoot actually exists and has the ability to move between the here and there, wherever *there* is, by simply going through the doorway through the dimensions. My experience in channeling with Mou has shown me just how little I understand about the world around us. ∞

CHAPTER 10

SECRET BEHIND

NAZI ROCKET TECHNOLOGY

One evening we were channeling with my alien guide, Mou, and I asked him if there was any conspiracy that he thought should be added to this book. He answered:

WE NEED TO LOOK AT WW2 AND THE GERMAN SCIENTISTS. WHY DID THEY KNOW SO MUCH ABOUT ROCKETS?

I was aware that the Nazi rocket research had far exceeded that of the Allies, but the United States developed the ultimate trump card, the atomic bomb. In my former book we talked about the wreck of an alien craft in 1938 in Bavaria where extraterrestrials survived and assisted the Germans in research. It had not sunk into my mind that the aliens had assisted in their rocket research. I asked him if their rapid rate of advancement was because of the 1938 crash. His answer was not quite what I expected.

BECAUSE THEY HELD THE CREW.

He had told us previously that the aliens were shape-shifters and blended in with the other humans. I asked him if this was accurate.

YES. THEY HELD THE GREAT COUNCIL HOSTAGE. IN THE END THAT SIDE LOST. IT WAS THE COUNCIL THAT BROUGHT THEM DOWN. TOO MUCH KNOWING WILL BITE YOU.

HISTORICAL BACKGROUND

In order to fully understand the rapid development of the German rocket program, let's take a look at the chronology of how Nazi Germany became the leader in what would become space exploration. After WWI, Germany was precluded by treaty from developing various types of military weapons. A loophole in the treaties did not stop them from developing rocket propelled craft. By 1930, a worldwide depression had Germany in its grip, and the Nazi party, under the leadership of Adolf Hitler, taking advantage of the unrest of the people, made wide political gains. From 1929 to 1932, the unemployment rate in

Germany had grown from 8% to 30% as industrial production dropped around 40%. Unrest among the people left the door open for radical political change. In 1932, Paul von Hindenburg was elected president at the age of eighty-four over Adolf Hitler. The ailing president appointed the leader of the Nazi party as chancellor, and the die was cast.

The year 1933 was a time when political events took place that would eventually lead to worldwide conflict. Hitler essentially took control of the government. Under his orders, the first concentration camp was constructed at Dachau, and Hermann Goering established the Gestapo. By August of 1934, von Hindenburg died, and Adolf Hitler became Fuhrer and seized all political power. Realizing the potential for rocket-propelled weapons, he supported their development.

Even before the Nazi party took complete control, the German Army made formal its rocket development program in August of 1932. By October of that year, Dr. Wernher von Braun, a thirty-three-year old brilliant scientist, joined the German Army Ordinance Office rocket program.

During this time, von Braun tested his first rocket in December 1932, which blew up on the launch pad, a failure. By December 1934, they developed and tested the A-2 rocket that flew a distance of 1.2 miles. In 1936, German scientists tested an A-3 rocket and, by 1939, had developed an A-5, weighing one ton, that climbed five miles before it burned out in a test. Tests were not indicative of a great rocket program. The point I am trying to make is that, by 1939, they were far from having a weapon capable of delivering a heavy payload over a long distance. In the relatively short time of three years, German technology in rocketry took a giant leap forward in capability.

By June 1942, Germany tested a prototype of the V-2 rocket that weighed 14 tons at takeoff, stood 47 feet in height ,and delivered a 2,150 warhead a maximum range of 200 miles, reaching a trajectory height of 60 miles and a speed of 3,300 mph. In only three years the capabilities of German rocketry had grown almost exponentially. By May 1943, the weapon was fully operational and over 100 were launched toward Poland. Something had occurred that allowed the Nazi scientists to advance their rocket program in such a manner. According to Mou, that help came in the form of alien assistance.

The V-2 rocket was an amazing weapon for its time. It stood 47 feet, had a diameter of 5.4 feet, and a loaded weight of 27,590 lbs. It had a range of 200 miles and flew as high as fifty-five miles, the first vehicle to enter outer space. In addition, the Germans developed a radio-control guidance system and launched them from mobile systems. This was truly an extraordinary system for its time, especially when you consider the majority of technological advances were made over a four-year period.

In another interesting historical side note, on March 15, 1944, Von Braun was arrested by the SS for concentrating more time and energy on space travel than he was for military weapons. Hitler later ordered him released because his services were considered indispensable to the doomed Nazi military effort. I guess if you

Nazi Germany V-2 rocket.
Courtesy Dollarphotoclub.

are associating with aliens that had to travel through space to get to Germany, you would develop a real interest in learning more about it. It would definitely be interesting to know the real story about how they knew so much about rockets.

A SOFT CRASH

Following up on his recommendation to write this chapter, I started the interview with Mou by asking him if the Nazi had shot down the space craft. My guess was that human technology at that time was incapable of hurting their space craft. His answer confirmed my belief:

NO, IT LOST POWER AND HAD TO LAND TO FIX THE PROBLEM, SOFT CRASH AND CREW OF 27.

The Germans had a lot of bargaining power if they held 27 aliens, including a member of the Great Council. I asked him to elaborate on the Great Council.

THIS COUNCIL IS VERY OLD AND WAS ESTABLISHED TO PROTECT PLANETS LIKE YOURS FROM INVASION. WE WATCH ALL THAT HAPPENS. YOU HAVE TO FOLLOW THE LAWS SET DOWN.

My assumption is that it was one of these members that was on the ship that crash landed. The council could not have been very happy one of its members was being held captive.

THE COUNCIL WAS PUT ON ALERT THAT AIRCRAFT HAD CRASHED AND IT'S MEMBERS WERE BEING HELD. THE COUNCIL SENT REPS TO RESCUE THEM. THE GERMAN GOVERNMENT TOLD US THAT WE COULD ONLY HAVE OUR MEMBERS BACK IF WE WOULD GIVE THEM INFORMATION ABOUT WHAT WE KNEW.

DON'T MESS WITH THE COUNCIL

The Nazis definitely had a lot of nerve trying to blackmail one of the most important and powerful organizations in the galaxy. I asked Mou how the council reacted to their demands. He replied:

THE COUNCIL DEBATED WHAT TO DO. WE HAVE CHEMICALS THAT SIMPLY KILL THOSE INVOLVED BUT WE DECIDED THAT IT WAS BETTER TO GIVE OUR OWN OLD TECH SUPPORT. SO WE HELPED EDUCATE THE CHOSEN SCIENTISTS THE KNOWLEDGE IN ROCKETRY. THE GERMANS WERE VERY ARROGANT AND HARD TO WORK WITH. WE ONLY INFORMED THEM OF THE ROOT THEORY INFORMATION.

Note that he said they were going to give old tech support to the Germans. I asked if they were giving aid to the Allies.

NOW ON THE OTHER SIDE WE WERE TEACHING ATOMIC KNOWLEDGE.

From our conversations I had the impression that the extraterrestrials were actually held forcibly against their will. With the great power available to the Great Council I wondered why they just did not come in and forcibly remove them from captivity. My next question addressed how the alien world reacted to their Great Council being held prisoner.

JUST A FIGURE OF SPEECH. THEY WERE NEVER PHYSICALLY HELD. THEY WERE WHAT YOU SAY, HELD OVER A BARREL. THEY WERE BETWEEN A ROCK AND A HARD SPOT. THE COUNCIL FELT BLACKMAILED.

No question that Mou was well familiar with all the human clichés. It must have been quite a threat if the Great Council felt blackmailed. I asked: "What threats were made by the Germans?"

WE WILL TELL THE WORLD ABOUT YOU. THEY FELT THAT THEY WERE BEING TOLD WHAT THEY MUST DO IN ORDER TO KEEP THE AGREEMENT. THEY DO NOT LIKE BEING TOLD WHAT TO DO. THEY TELL YOU WHAT YOU WILL DO. HITLER SAID YOU WILL AND THEY SAID NO WE WON'T AND THEN THEY SHOWED HITLER WHY YOU DO NOT BACK TALK. THAT IS WHY HE WAS FOUND DEAD.

To refresh your memory, the agreement he was referring to is the pact of secrecy where the aliens are allowed to observe humans and our governments keep the secret of their presence. Lucky for us that Hitler's ego and free will caused him to upset the Great Council. According to Mou, his arrogance cost him the war and his own life.

While the aliens were giving the Nazis old technological information, they were helping our side develop the atomic bomb. That seems like a fair trade off. Even though it was old technical information for the aliens, it was certainly new for the Germans. I inquired how the aliens were able to get along with the Nazi scientists.

THERE WERE FIVE OF THIRTY MEN WHO WERE OPEN. THEY WERE ABLE TO THINK THE INFORMATION FURTHER THAN WE SHOWED THEM.

I had originally believed the aliens were shape-shifters, so I asked Mou to describe what they looked like.

YOU, BUT WITH LARGE FOREHEADS, SMALL POINTY EARS AND SCALY SKIN.

This was not a type of alien description I had heard before. I asked him if they were like the reptilians.

KIND OF BUT THEY TOO GET LUMPED TOGETHER. ALL SCALY SKINS ARE NOT FROM THE SAME PLACE.

I guess I was comforted that not all scaly skins came from the same place. Since this was a type of extraterrestrial that was not familiar to me, I asked if they had a name.

I CANNOT SPELL IT RIGHT SO I WILL DO AS SOUNDS LIKE "FROGNOZITES."

THE RESCUE, OR NOT

In an earlier discussion, I had been told that the captives had been rescued. In my mind I was picturing a grand rescue attempt where alien special forces swooped in and saved the victims from the grasp of the bad guys, just like in the movies. When I asked how they were rescued he replied:

EMERGENCY CALL WENT TO US. THEY WERE IN CONTACT AT ALL TIMES. THEY SIMPLY MADE THE PARTS NEEDED AND FLEW HOME.

Are you telling me there was no rescue attempt?

NO, BUT WE DID FIX IT AND FLY IT OUT.

I must admit that explanation of the rescue was a bit of a letdown. When I asked if the Germans were allowed to inspect the inside of the space craft, he said:

YES, THEY WERE SHOWN THE POWER TECHNOLOGY BUT THEY JUST COULD NOT GET IT TO WORK WITH YOUR HEAVY METALS AT THAT TIME. THIS IS WHERE SPUN CARBONS COME FROM.

It is amazing how much of our modern technology comes from information given us by visitors from outer space. My last question inquired how long the aliens were held captive.

OH, LIKE 9 MONTHS.

I would think the German High Command would be a little upset that their captives escaped and they had irritated the most powerful ruling body in the galaxy. I asked Mou how the Nazis reacted after the escape of the extraterrestrials.

SHORTLY AFTER, THE GERMAN LEADERSHIP GOT PARANOID THINKING WE WOULD HELP THE OTHER SIDE COME BACK TO HARM THEM OR MANY OTHER THINGS. THIS IS WHEN THEY BEGAN TO LOSE THE WAR. THEY WERE MORE WORRIED ABOUT US.

I could see why the Germans would tend to look over their shoulders for fear of repercussions from their little hostage-taking program. As it turned out, they had more to fear from the might of the Allies and the Soviet Union closing in on their country. In the final months of the war, both sides had their eyes on the prize of the scientists who held the knowledge concerning the advanced Nazi weaponry. Our governments were now faced with a great conundrum: How could these men who provided the means of killing thousands, if not millions, of civilians not be treated as war criminals?

OPERATION PAPER CLIP

The job of laundering the history of the scientists was given to our Office of Strategic Services, better known as the OSS. Before the operation ended, over 1,500 Nazi scientists, engineers, technicians, and doctors were brought to the United States. It is interesting to point out that not only did we not want the information to go to the Soviet Union, they did not want them going to the United Kingdom. With the seed of the Cold War beginning, knowledge could rule the World. I asked him what happened to the scientists after the war.

WHEN THE WAR WAS OVER, TO SAVE THEIR LIVES THE SCIENTISTS TOLD OF THEIR LEARNING. SO THE USA LET THEM COME TO THE MAN TO WORK WITH WHAT THEY WERE SHOWN. THIS IS YOUR SPACE PROGRAM.

I asked if any of the Germans allowed to come to America after the war were really some of the aliens. He replied:

NO, THE COMMITTEE WOULD NOT PERMIT THEM TO STAY ON EARTH. THEY WERE RECALLED.

When I asked if the aliens helped us with rocket technology, his answer was:

NO, THE GERMANS KNEW THE TECHNOLOGY.

The grand scientific prize was Dr. Wernher von Braun. He had been the heart of the V-2 program and the best of the best. He was so bright that I asked Mou if he was an alien.

NO, VERY SMART MAN.

Score one for the human race. When I asked about Albert Einstein, he said his grandfather was a starman. At least von Braun was a very bright human who was not alien related. My next question inquired if he worked closely with the aliens while they were in Germany. Once again his answer contained a surprise.

YES, HE WENT TO SPACE TO SEE THINGS WORK.

No wonder he was more interested in space exploration than working on the Nazi weapons of mass destruction. One little problem for the United States was that von Braun was actually an SS officer, designer of a weapon that had been most effective killing civilians, and he should have been tried for war crimes. In spite of the fact that bringing these individuals to the United States was in violation of the Yalta and Potsdam agreements and President Truman's anti-Nazi order, false biographies and employment documents were made for the Germans. Our OSS even went so far as to expunge public records, affiliations, and memberships in troublesome organizations such as the SS. Once the paperwork was accomplished and the evidence of their past was gone, they were even given top-level security clearances in the United States. Clearly another situation where the ends justified the means. The project was given the name "Operation Paper Clip" because there were so many paper clips used to attach the fake documents to their files.

FROM NAZI TO FAME

Von Braun was flown to the United States where he was accepted with open arms into our fledgling space program. Moving to Alabama in 1952, he became director of the US Army Ordnance Guided Missile Project. His main responsibility was overseeing the launch of America's first earth satellite, Explorer 1, in 1958. By the time of this launch, he had even become a US citizen.

In 1960, he became director of the Marshall Space Flight Center where he developed the Saturn 1B and Saturn V space vehicle. The Saturn I rocket used for the Apollo 8 moon orbit in 1969 also came under his supervision. In 1972, he turned to private industry and became a vice president of the aerospace company Fairchild Industries. Not bad for a former SS officer. He died on June 16, 1977, truly the father of our space program. What he did not publicize is the fact that much of the knowledge was given to him by a bunch of aliens that happened to crash land in Germany and even took him for a ride in their space ship. ∞

WHAT HAPPENED

On Saturday, March 8, 2014, the greatest mystery in aeronautic history occurred over the Malay Peninsula. Malaysia Airlines Flight 370 with 12 crew members and 227 passengers from 15 different nations disappeared without a trace. It took off from the Kuala Lumpur International Airport in Malaysia headed for Beijing, China. Prior to disappearing from radar, there were no reports of bad weather, mechanical problems, or any distress signals that would indicate foul play aboard the Boeing 777. Last known contact with the plane indicated that the pilot changed course before dropping off the radar.

The event triggered the largest searches over land and sea in history. It began in the South China Sea and the Gulf of Thailand and ended over the vast expanses of the Indian Ocean. Analysis of satellite communications led to the conclusion that the plane ended up in the southern Indian Ocean.

Boeing 777 similar to Malaysian Flight 330.
Courtesy Dollarphotoclub.

The best guess is that the pilots flew the craft until it ran out of gas and then crashed it into the Indian Ocean west of Australia. Investigators concluded that the passengers were probably killed by decompression of the cabin at a high altitude. The lack of oxygen and pressurization would have taken the lives of the cabin crew and passengers in less than a minute. If any humans know what happened to the plane and crew, they are not talking. From almost the beginning of the event I asked the Heavenly guides what was taking place. As you will see, the disappearance was part of a huge conspiracy.

I started seeking information about the disappearance of the Malaysian flight in the beginning of April 2014, less than a month after the event, while all the countries were in a search frenzy. I started by asking a master guide what happened to the Malaysian airliner. His reply fit right in with the theme of this book, he stated:

CONSPIRACY.

I asked if the plane crashed but did not receive an answer. When I inquired if it landed safely, he replied:

YES.

It is not exactly easy to hide a Boeing 777. They have a wingspan of 200 feet and a length of 242 feet. It is almost inconceivable that an object of that size could be hidden from our modern surveillance satellites and equipment. When I asked where it landed, the guide stated:

COAST, VERY RURAL.

It would have to be very rural to hide such an object. When I asked the current location of the airplane he said:

ISLAND.

My next question was about the location of the island. To my surprise he was quite specific.

OFF VIETNAM. 500 MILES OFF THE VIETNAM COAST.

If you check out the map of the South China Sea you will see there are several groups of isolated islands that could meet the description. There were a total of 239 individuals, including the pilots and crew, on board who were never accounted for. I asked if the passengers were dead. His answer was what I expected.

SADLY, YES.

Were the pilots involved?

YES, SEVERAL INVOLVED.

When I asked if the plane was taken by terrorists, his answer came as no surprise.

YES. NO GAS. IT WAS FORCED DOWN BEFORE DESTINATION WAS REACHED.

The plane supposedly had a lot of fuel on board. I asked the intended destination for the hijacked airplane.

PAKISTAN, IRAN.

That answer was what I expected, the usual cast of characters. I was curious to find out what their plans were for the plane.

FLY DESTRUCTIVE WEAPONS.

Destructive weapons can include a large slew of objects. When I inquired if they were going to fill it with bombs, his answer indicated a worst case scenario.

NUCLEAR MATERIAL.

The thought of a Boeing 777 filed with nuclear material is enough to make anyone nervous. If the plane had not been forced to land before its destination, someone was in for a rude surprise. Next I asked the intended target.

CHINA, ISRAEL, UNITED STATES.

This session took place less than a month after the disappearance. I asked if the plane would ever be found.

YES. IT MAY END UP IN PARTS IN THE OCEAN.

Note that, in May 2014, we were told that parts of the plane would end up in the ocean. With that answer I ended the portion of the session that dealt with the airliner. That part of the prediction came true in August 2015 when a section of a wing flap was found on the Reunion Islands, a French possession in a remote part of the Indian Ocean. As of the publication of this book, no major portions of the wreckage have been located.

During the next month, all the news channels were obsessed with the story as other countries, including the United States, joined in the search. In spite of the searchers using the best high-tech equipment in the world, there was no confirmed contact or wreckage debris found.

I took from that comment that if it was ever found, the public would never find out about it. The next time we discussed the event was a channeling session in the middle of June, four months after the disappearance. In spite of the herculean search effort, including a special submarine from the United States, there was still no trace of the Boeing 777. When I asked the guide if it was still on the island, his answer was:

NO, IN PIECES.

When I asked where the pieces were currently located his response was:

PAKISTAN.

I don't think that answer should surprise anyone. They are probably using our foreign aid to put the plane back together. Next, I asked if Pakistan was behind the hijacking of the plane.

TERRORISTS FROM DIFFERENT AREAS.

I find it inconceivable that the United States is not aware of an operation of this size. We spend billions on satellites and equipment that I've never even heard of to keep track of events like this. I asked if the United States had any idea what happened to the plane.

NOT ENTIRELY.

I have no idea what he meant by that statement. It sounds like there is the possibility of some complicity with what happened to the Boeing 777. The next time I checked in with the guides to see how the conspiracy was progressing was in the middle of October. Seven months had expired since the incident. I started by asking if the plane would ever be found.

ALREADY FORGOTTEN.

Unfortunately, I think his statement was sad but quite true. Most of the search vessels had been pulled off and they were talking about some fancy equipment that could trace the bottom and perhaps pick up the wreckage. I asked if this new search was a cover up.

IT ALL IS.

Are you saying that all of the searches were a cover up?

YES.

It would be very sad to think that so much energy, time, and money would be expended in a cover up. I inquired where the plane was currently located.

SHIFTED.

I told him that I thought the plane was still in Pakistan. He verified my previous information.

IT WAS.

Notice that his answer was in the past tense. I inquired if it was in Iran.

NO.

Next, I asked if it was in Afghanistan.

NO.

It was becoming obvious the guide was not going to disclose the current location of the plane. Wherever it was, I wanted to know if it was still going to be used as a bomb.

UNDECIDED AT THIS TIME.

What is the reason for the plane's disappearance?

TERROR. TERRORIST MOTIVES.

In the beginning of May 2015, we were conducting a channeling session with another master guide. I attempted to reaffirm what happened to the plane, so I inquired if it had crashed. Our guide reaffirmed what we had learned a month earlier with a single word:

NO.

Next, I inquired if the plane was currently in one piece. He replied:

NO.

When I asked if it was being disassembled, his answer was:

YES.

The massive scale of the conspiracy was beginning to sink in. I asked if all this was taking place according to a master plan.

YES.

In my mind, this type of operation could only be conducted by a nation or state. His reply started to confirm how diabolical and complex our world has become. He met my question with a question of his own.

COUNTRY OR GROUP?

Was it Al Qaeda?

YES.

We had been told in an earlier session that the plane had landed on an island west of Vietnam. I asked if it was still on the island.

DISTRIBUTED ELSEWHERE.

If the hijackers were going to such an extent to dismantle the plane and ship the parts elsewhere, there certainly was an ulterior plan. I asked if they intending to rebuild it to fly again. His answer was not overly comforting.

FUTURE.

The idea that a huge airplane could disappear, be disassembled, put back together to fly again was a bit overwhelming. My suspicions were confirmed when I inquired if the Malaysian flight would ever be found.

NOT IN PUBLIC VIEW.

A MUCH DIFFERENT VERSION

In the winter of 2015, the missing airliner had disappeared from the headlines. During a channeling session with my alien spirit friend, I brought up the subject of the missing Malaysian 777. Thinking that I might be able to find the location of where the terrorists would have buried the bodies, I asked him what had happened to the remains of the passengers. I was definitely not prepared for his answer.

BLUES TOOK THEM OFF.

Are you talking about blue aliens, like yourself?

YES.

We had been told by earlier guides that terrorists had hijacked the missing plane and that the passengers had been killed. I asked him if the passengers were alive.

MOST, UFO MID-AIR COLLISION.

That answer caught me off guard. I though the plane was hijacked by terrorists?

RIGHT, I THINK IF I AM NOT MISTAKEN IT WAS PART OF THE EASTERN UNREST, BUT IT WAS A MID-AIR CRASH.

Just to be clear, you are saying the Malaysian 777 had a mid-air collision with a UFO after it was hijacked.

YES.

In a previous session we were told that the plane was hijacked by terrorists, the passengers killed, and the plane dismantled. You just told us the plane collided with an alien ship. Why the two stories?

SAME.

I was having a hard time seeing how the two renditions of the plane incident were the same. I told him that the other guide told us that the plane was dismantled and he just told us the plane was sunk. How is that the same thing?

SAME.

I could see I was not making a lot of progress on this line of questioning. I asked who hit who?

IT WAS A MISHAP.

Where is the wreckage?

SUNK.

Where is it sunk?

WHERE IT CANNOT BE FOUND. THEY SUNK IT BY ONE OF THE UFO BASES. HIDE YOUR MISTAKES!

That was a loaded answer! He just clearly said they had UFO bases deep under the ocean. I guess it is good to know that aliens make mistakes, much like humans. He had said earlier that the blues took most of the passengers off the ship. I asked if the passengers would ever be returned.

NOPE, THEY ARE HAPPY IN THEIR NEW HOME PLACE.

He had mentioned that the blues were from a planet in the far arm of the Milky Way. My next question was if they took the passengers to their home planet.

NO.

If you did not take them to your planet, where did you take them?

ONE MOON OFF JUPITER. A PLACE NOT UNLIKE EARTH. IT IS ON THE BACK SIDE. YOU HAVE TO LOOK BACK AT IT.

He seemed really confident in that answer. Who was going to argue with him that you had to look back to see the moon? Are you telling us the plane will be lost forever?

YES, MAY BE ABLE TO SEE A BODY PIECE BY UNMANNED SUB, BUT NOT FOR YEARS.

I asked if he could tell us the location of where the remains of the ship were sunk to the bottom of the ocean.

NOPE. 27 DEGREES NORTH OF SANTA CLAUS.

Did I ever mention before that my alien spirit friend can be a smart-ass? There is no way he is going to even hint at the location of the airplane.

In late September 2015, I thought I would attempt to update the information we had been given concerning Flight 370. This would be the last opportunity for information since this book was ready to go to the publisher. Several months earlier a piece of the flap assembly was found on a remote island in the Indian Ocean. I started by asking if the part of the airplane that was found was planted.

YES.

Why was the part planted?

MISDIRECTION.

I was still having a hard time believing that the aliens were responsible for hiding the airplane in the sea. I inquired if the aliens planted the wing part.

YES.

Where is the 777 today?

SEA.

What country is it the closest to?

AUSTRALIA.

Is that where the aliens put it?

YES.

His answers verified the information given in previous sessions. Let me attempt to give a summary of what we are told happened to Malaysian Flight 370 as told to us by both human and alien guides. In the beginning, the flight was hijacked by terrorists. It was taken to a hidden landing place off the coast of Vietnam. Parts of the airplane were planted in the Indian Ocean to be found at a later time and to make the public think that the 777 had crashed somewhere in the Indian Ocean. While the plane was being moved by the terrorists, it collided with an alien craft. Attempting to cover their mistake, the aliens sunk the ship in a deep part of the Ocean near one of the underwater UFO bases. As a distraction, they planted a part of the plane on a remote island. The final resting place for the plane is close to Australia. The passengers were removed from the ship at the time of the collision with the extraterrestrial ship by blue aliens and taken to one of the moons of Jupiter where they must remain.

I told you at the beginning of the book that you would read things in this book that would stretch your imagination to the limit and I believe this chapter is one of them. There is no doubt it has stretched mine. ∞

CHAPTER 12

THE LEGEND

OF BILLY THE KID

Anyone interested in the colorful history of the American Old West has heard the name of the famous young outlaw known as William H. Bonney or Billy the Kid. As the legend goes, by the age of twenty-one, the young man had killed twenty-one men in cold blood. He was hunted down and shot by Pat Garrett, a US Marshall. No photographs were taken of the corpse and "the Kid" was buried in a grave the same day of his demise.

The historical version seemed quite cut and dry until a ninety-two-year-old man living under the name of Brushy Bill Roberts came forward in the late 1940s and claimed that he was Billy the Kid and Pat Garrett had shot the wrong man in the back. An investigative reporter spent months interviewing the individual, and the old man even talked with other survivors of the Lincoln County Wars who had actually been acquaintances of the outlaw during his short career. The survivors agreed that the old man was indeed the Kid. Roberts even exhibited twenty-six scars of wounds similar to those of the Kid.

A GUIDE SPEAKS OF BILLY THE KID

One evening we were channeling with our guide, Raz, and I asked him if Pat Garrett killed the famous outlaw, Billy the Kid? He replied:

No.

With that answer, my hopes for a very interesting chapter soared. When I asked if I could reach the spirit of Billy the Kid, my aspirations were momentarily dashed on the rocks of reality. His answer to that question was:

No.

Generally, spirits are quite eager to have their stories told. I figured there had to be a reason why we could not contact the spirit of Billy the Kid. I inquired if his soul had reincarnated and was presently back on Earth in an incarnate body.

Yes.

So the soul of Billy the Kid has returned and is on a new life path. Since he was preoccupied in such a way, the only source of information into the true facts was to ask Raz, our intermediary. Keep in mind that the guides have an amazing ability to view past events. I asked our guide if he would be willing to give me the information I needed to do this chapter and his answer was:

YES.

SOME HISTORIC BACKGROUND

Before delving into the details of the conspiracy, let me start by telling the story as recorded in the history books. The famous outlaw was actually born in New York City on November 23, 1859. His real name was William Henry McCarty Jr. Little is known about his early life, but it is believed that the family was deserted by the father and his mother migrated westward in an attempt to find a way to support Henry and his brother. His mother died of tuberculosis when he was fifteen, leaving Henry and his brother to fend for themselves in a very dangerous environment.

In order to survive, the pair turned to minor thievery, and the die was cast for his supposed short life of crime. Leaving his brother to fend for himself, the kid became involved in cattle rustling and joined a gang of hardened criminals known as "the boys." McCarty did not realize that he was about to become involved in a very violent event in western history known as the Lincoln County Wars. Billy the Kid would emerge from the war an outlaw and wanted man.

THE LINCOLN COUNTY WAR

In the 1870s, Lincoln County was a huge hunk of real estate in New Mexico. This was cattle country, and towns were few and far between. Wealthy ranchers Lawrence Murphy and James Dolan gained political control of the county and maintained a virtual monopoly over the sale of dry goods through Murphy's general store. The sheriff of the town was also under their control.

An English-born newcomer to the county, John Tunstall, with business partners Alexander McSween and cattleman John Chisum, decided to put an end to the monopoly and open their own dry goods store in 1876. Both sides began to hire lawmen and ranch hands, and established outlaw gangs loyal to their respective sides. The Murphy/Dolan side featured Lincoln County Sheriff Brand and a bunch of outlaws known as the Jesse Evans Gang. Opposing them was the Tunstall/McSween/Chisum group that hired their own group of outlaws, and their own lawmen in the form of town constable Richard Brewer and Deputy US Marshall Robert Widenmann. The young man known now as Billy the Kid joined the Tunstall group, which had assumed the name "the Regulators."

Each side began to harass and rustle the other sides' cattle. By February

The only known image of Billy the Kid.
Courtesy US Archives.

1878, the Murphy/Dolan side, in a court case that was later dismissed, used their political influence to obtain a court order to seize the other side's assets. Sheriff Brady, an ally of Murphy/Dolan, formed a posse to seize McSween's assets. The Jesse Evans gang of hardened gunfighters was part of the posse.

The posse caught up with Tunstall on Feburary 18, 1878, while the Englishman and several of his ranch hands, including Billy the Kid, were rounding up strays. Instead of arresting Tunstall, Jesse Evans and several other members of the gang killed him in cold blood. Billy and several others observed the murder from a distance but, because of the size of the posse, could do nothing about it at the time. Bonney/the Kid had become very close to Tunstall and vowed revenge. This was the beginning of the violence known as the Lincoln County War.

The Regulators found a justice of the peace friendly to the Tunstall side who actually deputized the group of outlaws now hell bent on revenge. By March 9th, the Regulators had managed to capture and in some cases execute all of the individuals involved in the murder of Tunstall. Sheriff Brady, now on the side that was getting killed, realized he had a problem and requested that the Governor of New Mexico intervene. The Governor decreed that the justice of the peace friendly to the Tunstills had no authority to deputize the Regulators, thereby removing the cloak of legal protection from the Regulators and leaving Sheriff Brady the only lawman in Lincoln County.

WHO SHOT THE SHERIFF?

Not at all discouraged by their lack of legal protection, six of the Regulators, including the Kid, decided they would attack Sheriff Brady and his deputies in front of Tunstall's store on April 1, 1878. The sheriff died of lead poison from twelve or more gunshot wounds, and another of his deputies was also killed. McCarty, or Billy the Kid, was wounded during the gunfight but recovered from the wounds. Needless to say, the killing of two official lawmen did not go over well with the governor.

The two sides continued to kill each other in multiple skirmishes until the final confrontation on July 18 that came to be known as the battle of Lincoln, New Mexico. Around fifty Regulators took up positions around the town of Lincoln with the majority defending the McSween house and the Ellis store. The Kid was one of the defenders of the McSween house. The town was surrounded by the Dolan/Murphy bunch as well as a group of outlaws known as the Seven Rivers cowboys.

Fighting continued over the next three days as both sides swore and took shots at each other. It was not until the US Cavalry arrived and pointed their cannon at the Ellis store that the participants in that location realized the battle was over. As I mentioned before, Kid was one of those defending the McSween house that at that time was looking at the muzzle of a US military cannon.

In the late afternoon, the Murphy/Dolan side set fire to the McSween house, in spite of the fact that there were several women and five children in the house. By 9 p.m., the fire had spread to the point that the men inside had to attempt an escape. Billy the Kid and several of his associates ran from the house firing their weapons with return fire coming from the Dolan's. In the melee, several Regulators were killed, but the Kid managed to escape. He was on the run again, a fugitive from the law.

SCREWED BY THE GOVERNOR

As government intervention forced calm to once again come to Lincoln County, the Kid attempted to gain a pardon from the governor by testifying against many of the Lincoln County War participants. As part of his agreement, he turned himself in and testified against several defendants. Instead of being a free man, the governor reneged on the agreement and left town without giving him the promised pardon. Billy the Kid remained a wanted man in spite of his attempt to clear his name. His guards seemed to realize that he had been double crossed and essentially let the Kid walk out of his jail with no violence. Billy the Kid was once again on the run as a wanted man and continued to rustle cattle and live the life of an outlaw. Since his old enemies, the Dolans, were now in charge of the county, the Kid was blamed for many events in which he played no part. His fame grew as a brutal killer and outlaw, some of it deserved.

During this time, a cowboy by the name of Pat Garrett ran for sheriff of Lincoln County knowing one of his first jobs would be to capture the now-famous outlaw Billy the Kid. Garrett was elected on November 2, 1880. On November 27, a posse headed by Deputy James Carlyle surrounded the Kid and his gang at the Greathouse Ranch. In a gunfight that ensued, Deputy Carlyle was killed by his own men, but the Kid was blamed for the murder. As a result of him being blamed for the killing of a deputy marshal, pressure grew for his arrest. On December 14, Sheriff Garrett formed a posse to capture the Kid, who now had a $500 reward on his head. The purchasing power of that amount today would be around $12,000. By December 23, they managed to surround the Kid and, after a short gun fight, he and his gang surrendered. By New Year's Day, they were transported to Santa Fe where they were placed in jail. It was decided they would be tried for the murder of Sheriff Brady whose shooting occurred at the beginning of the Lincoln County War.

On April 9, 1881, the Kid was found guilty of the murder of Sheriff Brady and ordered to be hung on May 13. It is interesting to note that of all the individuals tried for the killing and shooting during the Lincoln County War, Billy the Kid was the only one convicted and sentenced to death. By 10 p.m. the same day, he was taken by stage coach to Lincoln where his sentence was to be carried out. On April 21, he arrived in Lincoln and was placed in a room in the courthouse, chained to a corner of the room.

The trip to Lincoln, New Mexico, had taken five days. One of the guards on the trip, Bob Orlinger, had been a member of Dolan gang and apparently harassed the Kid throughout the trip. He continued to guard and harass the Kid while he was confined at the courthouse in Lincoln. Garrett ordered that two deputies were to be with the Kid twenty four hours a day until he was hung. On April 28, the guards on duty were Olinger and Deputy James Bell.

ON THE ROAD AGAIN

At lunch time, Olinger left to escort the other prisoners across the street to have their meal at the hotel, leaving Bell in charge of the Kid, who would be fed in the room at the courthouse. Realizing this was his best opportunity to escape, he convinced Deputy Bell to allow him to use the outhouse behind the courthouse. Bell unchained him from the chair but left the Kid in leg irons and wrist manacles. Apparently, the Kid had a double-jointed thumb that allowed him to pull his hand free of the hand cuff. With his hands free, he grabbed Deputy Bell's hand gun and when the deputy attempted to run, killed him with his own weapon.

Deputy Olinger heard the gunshot from across the street and rushed toward the courthouse. By this time, the Kid had grabbed Olingers shotgun and was standing on the porch, taking careful aim at the chest of the deputy. According to witnesses, the last words Olinger heard was the Kid saying "Hello Bob" as he fired both barrels into his chest. The Kid saddled a horse and rode out of town without any interference. Needless to say he was now on the top of Garrett's most-wanted list.

Instead of leaving the country, the Kid stayed in New Mexico with friends, apparently having little fear of being captured. He was quite a lady's man and spent time visiting with the local females, dancing and partying. One of his girlfriends was Paulita Maxwell, the sister of Pete Maxwell, who owned a ranch near Fort Sumner, New Mexico. The older Maxwell did not like the idea of his sister hanging out with a hardened criminal. Acting on a tip, probably from Maxwell, Pat Garrett and two deputies headed to Fort Sumner with the intent of capturing Billy the Kid, dead or alive.

SHOT IN THE BACK

According to the story told by Garrett, On July 14, the Sheriff went to the Maxwell ranch and entered the bedroom where Maxwell was sleeping. He woke up Maxwell to inquire if he had seen the Kid. While the sheriff was inquiring as to his whereabouts, the Kid was staying with a friend nearby. The outlaw decided to come to the Maxwell house to obtain a piece of fresh meat from a yearling that had recently been slaughtered and was hanging at the ranch. The Kid noticed the other two deputies in the dark and backed into Pete Maxwell's bedroom with a gun and knife in hand, asking who the two people were hiding in the dark. Garrett fired two shots, hitting Billy the Kid in the back and killing him instantly.

Hearing the gunshots, the residents came out and realized the famous outlaw had been killed. Garrett allowed the residents to take the body to the local carpenter shop where the body was cleaned and dressed. A wake was performed and the body was laid to rest in the local boot hill by noon the same day. The death certificate created by a local justice of the peace was signed but never officially registered. Garrett went on to publish a book in which the Kid was vilified and made a outlaw legend of the old west. And so ended the story of Billy the Kid, until 1948.

ALIVE AND KICKING AT NINETY-TWO

In an event totally unrelated to the legend of Billy the Kid, a probate investigator named William Morrison was working on a land dispute case of an elderly man named Joe Hines in Florida. The year was 1948. In a conversation, Morrison admitted that he was really Jessie Evans of the Lincoln County/Dalton gang fame. After being released from prison in 1882, he decided to "go straight." Coincidentally, the investigator was related to the Maxwell family of Ft. Sumner. As the conversation moved on to where Pat Garrett killed the Kid, Hines/Evans stated that the Kid was still living! He even gave Billy's current alias as Ollie Roberts and he still lived in Hamilton, Texas. His nickname was "Brushy Bill." I guess "Billy the Kid" would have been too obvious.

Morrison began to write letters to Roberts and managed to arrange a meeting in June of 1949. At first "Brushy Bill" said that Billy the Kid was really his half-brother living in Mexico. When pressed to go to Mexico for an interview, he finally conceded that he really was the long thought-to-be dead famous outlaw known as Billy the Kid. When the investigator asked Brushy Bill to prove he really was the famous outlaw, he removed his clothes and pointed out twenty-six knife and bullet scars on his body, many of which corresponded to wounds incurred at various times by the Kid. The real Kid had the ability to slip off manacles from his hands. If you remember he made his jail break where he killed a deputy and Bob Olinger by slipping from handcuffs. When asked to demonstrate how he slipped off the handcuffs, Brushy Bill showed that he had a double jointed thumb that allowed him to make his hands smaller than his wrists. There was an awful lot of circumstantial evidence.

ANOTHER VERSION OF THE SHOOTING
OF BILLY THE KID

When Brushy Bill gave his account of the night Pat Garrett claimed to have killed the Kid, the story was a little bit different. The night of the shooting, Billy was coming from a dance with a young friend named Billy Barlow. Arriving in Fort Sumner late at night, they actually got word that Garrett and his posse were in town. The Kid and his buddy went to a friends' house where he knew they would be safe. The friend began to prepare some beans for dinner but had no meat. They were aware that Maxwell had a freshly slaughtered cow at his house and they were welcome to have some of the meat. Billy the Kid sensed a trap, but Barlow grabbed a knife and went to the Maxwell house to cut a slab of meat. Barlow had no idea that Garrett and his deputies were at the Maxwell house.

When the Kid heard several shots from the Maxwell house, he grabbed two pistols and ran toward the sound of the gunfire. As he approached the gate of the house, he saw the shadows of the deputies and began firing at them. As the deputies returned fire, he was hit in the lower left jaw, losing a tooth. As he turned to run, he was hit in the left shoulder. As he escaped over the fence, he was grazed in the forehead by another bullet. A Mexican woman took him in and bandaged his wound. The Kid heard that Garrett had shot his friend Billy Barlow in the back and was passing off the body as that of the Kid. The sheriff knew that he had killed an innocent man by shooting him in the back and the only way to save his hide was to make the world think he had killed the famous outlaw. Billy realized that with the law considering him dead, he had to leave the area once and for all. He went to Mexico and began a new life that even included a stint with Bill Cody's Wild West Show.

When in doubt of the facts concerning an issue, we generally turn to one of our guides for answers. When I asked if Brushy Bill Roberts was actually Billy the Kid, the guide replied:

YES.

My next question asked if Pat Garrett killed an innocent man, he replied:

YES.

According to our guide, on that night in 1881, Pat Garrett shot an innocent man in the back and saved his own butt by passing off the innocent man's death as that of Billy the Kid. In this instance we were not able to contact the real spirit of the Kid for confirmation because he had reincarnated, and his soul is somewhere among us. My guess is he is probably a law man this time around. ∞

CHAPTER 13

THE KILLING OF CAMELOT

WHO MURDERED JFK?

In this chapter I will explore the possible theories concerning the assassination of President John Fitzgerald Kennedy by asking questions of the heavenly guides as well as the spirit of JFK. After all, who would be more qualified to discuss the killing of our American President than the spirit of the victim? One evening in November, just days before the anniversary of his death, the spirit of John Kennedy appeared to Barbara Lee and myself at one of our channeling sessions. His answers, as well as those of other heavenly guides, have given me an in-depth look at the events that led up to and included his murder, the planners and perpetrators, and the subsequent cover-up.

Perhaps no incident in the history of our country has generated more theories of conspiracy than the assassination of the thirty-fifth president of the United States, John Kennedy. Those of us old enough to have experienced the emotion of November 22, 1963, can relate where they were when they heard the news that Kennedy was killed. In my minds' eye I can still see little John Jr. saluting his father's casket. In an instant, the moral direction of our country was changed forever.

According to official government reports, a single shooter using an Italian bolt action rifle killed the most powerful man in the world while riding in an open automobile down a street in Dallas, Texas, surrounded by the Secret Service and Dallas police. The killer was then shot by a grief-stricken owner of a strip club with ties to organized crime, who then in turn died in jail from cancer. In the aftermath of the shooting, multiple witnesses to the shooting died of suicide or mysterious causes. A famous journalist, Dorothy Kilgallen, died suddenly after having an in-depth interview with Jack Ruby, the killer of Oswald, the designated official assassin. How could anyone in their right mind doubt the official government story? It is now over fifty years since the murder of President Kennedy and over sixty percent of the American people still think there was a hidden conspiracy.

As if there wasn't enough tragedy in the Kennedy family, on July 16, 1999, John Jr. and his wife were killed in the wreck of a small plane off Martha's Vineyard. The "official" probable cause was deemed to be pilot error: "Kennedy's failure to maintain control of the airplane during a descent over water at night, which was a result of spatial disorientation." Apparently he was not qualified to fly a plane by instruments only. It needs to be pointed out that other pilots flying similar routes reported no visual horizon due to haze and the crash occurred in conditions not legally requiring the use of instruments. I think you can see where I am going with this part of the chapter.

The 1950s and '60s represented a far different time and mindset than we see today. The bloody Korean War had ended with an Armistice Agreement in 1953. By the early 1960s the Strategic Air Command was keeping nuclear armed bombers in the air at all times to respond to a sneak attack. Russia, under the direction of Nikita Khrushchev, was deeply involved in a cold war with the United States and our allies that threatened to become a hot war at any time. The Russian leader made the statement "we will bury you" and was well on the way when he placed missiles in Cuba that were capable of delivering nuclear warheads as far as New York City.

Fidel Castro had taken over control of Cuba, and there was now a heavily armed Communist nation, with close ties to Russia, within shouting distance of Miami. During this time, the Central Intelligence Agency was heavily involved in attempting to overthrow unfriendly governments and even kill their leaders. Our country had a lot of enemies, and you did not have to look far away to find them.

Dwight Eisenhower, our president at the time, gave the CIA orders to develop an army consisting of individuals who had fled Cuba and wanted to overthrow Castro. When Kennedy was inaugurated, he inherited the scheme. In April 1961, several months after the inauguration, a force of 1,400 Cuban ex-patriots landed at the Bay of Pigs in an attempt to overthrow the Castro government by force. The CIA botched the air support part of the mission assuring that the Cuban government troops took over 1,100 of the attacking troops as prisoners. Needless to say, the Castro government was quite upset that the United States invaded their country. At the same time, the free Cuban immigrants, most of whom lived in the Miami area and now had relatives in Cuban jails, were upset that our president had canceled the air cover, and the invasion had failed. There was no shortage of Cubans on both sides of the Straits of Florida who had motive to assassinate President Kennedy.

Not to be outdone by the CIA, the joint chiefs came up with a plan called "Operation Northwood" that would incite the American public to endorse an attack on Cuba and remove the Communist regime. Documents obtained by the Freedom of Information Act show that the joint chiefs of staff prepared plans, approved by President Eisenhower, to carry out a false flag series of terrorist acts against our own country. American agents, disguised as Castro representatives, would carry out bloody attacks to trick the American public into supporting an invasion of Cuba. When Kennedy became president, he vetoed the operation to the chagrin of the joint chiefs. In the 1960s, it is a proven fact that our military was willing to kill American citizens in order to gain support for an invasion of Cuba!

Lyndon Baines Johnson was a senator from Texas with an unsavory past who wanted to be president of the United States. He had been involved with accusations of political payoffs as well as accused of stuffing ballot boxes in Texas to assure his elections. Some even whispered of the possibility of the mysterious deaths of political opponents. Possessing a volatile temper, he was also rumored to have ties to organized crime. When it came time for Jack Kennedy to select a running mate in 1960, Lyndon Johnson was far from being on the top of the vice president list. Unfortunately for the Kennedys, if Johnson could not be president, he certainly wanted to be vice president and was willing to use his contacts to achieve his goal.

Jack Kennedy was troubled with severe back pain and suffered from Addison's disease. As a result, he was treated with pain killers and steroid shots. One of the steroid's used happened to be testosterone. You can't watch current television commercials without knowing the effect of testosterone. The soon-to-be president took advantage of the steroid on many occasions, not necessarily with his wife nearby.

The patriarch of the family, Joseph P. Kennedy, had created a family fortune by investing in stocks and the importing of whiskey. Mafia boss Frank Costello bragged of being involved with him in bootlegging operations. He was active in the movie industry and had a long-term affair with actress Gloria Swanson. A piece of advice given to his sons was to never pass up getting laid, and I don't think that meant taking a nap. The Kennedy boys took this advice to heart and tried to follow their father's advice at every opportunity. Being married had little effect on their activities. As a result, the first Catholic candidate for president of the United States may have had a few problems with his background that had implications with the voting public. The America of the 1960s had not as yet gone through the sexual revolution we see today.

J. Edgar Hoover, a closet homosexual, was the head of the FBI and had a few things in his background that he also wanted to keep secret. Lyndon Johnson was a longtime friend of Hoover's and was not adverse to using blackmail to advance his political future. Johnson had Hoover explain to Kennedy the downside of not having the Texan on the ticket, and a political marriage was created—a little bit like finding out your one-night-stand is pregnant. By 1963, there was open hostility between the Kennedys and the Johnsons in the White House. In a meeting with select reporters at the White house, Bobby Kennedy told the reporters that the vice president was fair game for their articles. The president was quoted as saying that there would be a new vice president during the next term. Time was running out for Lyndon Baines Johnson and his political aspirations to be President.

As soon as Jack Kennedy was elected, he appointed his brother Bobby as attorney general. For the first time in decades, the federal government began to aggressively prosecute organized crime. As head of the FBI, J. Edgar Hoover had practiced a hands-off policy and was actually rumored to have ties to the underworld. Apparently, the Mafia had photographs that were taken one night when he was out of the closet that Hoover felt should remain a secret.

In addition, the organized crime families were not responding well to finding their members behind bars. It was also rumored that the CIA was involved in drug running to fund its black operations that were conducted without congressional oversight. Pressure on the organized crime members conducting the drug operations would have a very adverse effect on funding CIA secret activities. If the agency was truly involved with the Mafia, they certainly had access to the top mobsters.

As if there were not enough enemies wandering around the Hemisphere, the president began to realize the futility of fighting Communism in an obscure nation named Vietnam. In 1961, he had agreed to send 1,000 advisors to train the South Vietnamese army. Charles De Gaulle warned Kennedy that warfare in Vietnam would trap America in a "bottomless military and political swamp." Even though the joint chiefs were salivating over the opportunity to fight a new war, the new president was beginning to understand that this might not be the time to draw a preverbial red line. Needless to say, the defense contractors were less than overjoyed at the prospect of not being able to sell billions of dollars to the military for their toys of war. Kennedy's unique concept of trying to do what was right for the American people had certainly generated enough enemies capable of putting together one hell of a conspiracy!

The process of generating the information for this chapter took place over a period of several months where I would ask for a master guide and present him with questions about the assassination. Sessions would generate more questions with the process culminating in my requesting the appearance of the spirit of John Kennedy one evening as we approached the fiftieth anniversary of his murder. He appeared and was very anxious to tell us the events surrounding the murder. His answers verified the previous information that was supplied by the guides.

DETAILS OF THE ASSASSINATION

On the first evening of seeking the truth concerning the Kennedy murder, I asked the master guide if Oswald killed the president. His reply was:

NO, HE DID NOT.

It appears that the sixty percent of Americans who believe the Kennedy assassination was a conspiracy are correct! When I asked the spirit of the president if Oswald fired the shot that killed him the reply was:

NO.

There seems to be unanimous agreement on the other side that Lee Harvey Oswald was framed for the killing of our thirty-fifth president. I asked the guide how many shots were fired and the answer was:

5.

Next I asked if Oswald fired a shot and the answer from the guide was:

YES, HE MISSED.

The Warren report claimed the number of shots fired were four, and they were all from Oswald's bolt action rifle. When I asked JFK how many shots were fired his answer was "5." It appears that two of the shooters fired at the same moment and the crack of the guns were heard as a single shot. Another possibility is that one of the guns had a silencer. He went on to say that there were five shooters involved. The conspirators provided ample backup to assure the success of the mission. I went on to ask the president if Oswald was in the Book Depository Building and he replied:

YES.

When I asked if Oswald fired and missed his answer was:

HE WAS AWAY IN ANOTHER AREA.

Oswald said he was in another part of the building having lunch. It appears as though the killing of Kennedy was a well-orchestrated event with multiple shooters in different locations in case the initial shooters failed to hit their target. My first inquiry into the location and identity of the shooters began when I asked the guide what the two men were doing behind the fence on the grassy knoll. His reply was:

YOU ARE WISE, ONE OTHER.

I am always happy to accept a compliment from a guide. Where was the other shooter?

STORM DRAIN.

My guess is that by the time the automobile carrying the president got to the storm drain, there was no need of additional shots. At a later session, I inquired of the spirit of JFK the location of the fatal shot and he replied:

TWO SHOTS.

I think he misunderstood my question and told me how many shots hit him. Next I asked the former President if one was from the grassy knoll and he replied:

YES.

Was the fatal shot fired from the grassy knoll? His reply came as a surprise. It was:

NO, ON THE ROOF.

In all of my research I never saw any suggestion that there was a shooter on the roof of the Book Depository Building. It would make sense to have the kill shot come from a similar trajectory to that of the sixth-floor window where Oswald was supposedly located.

THE SHOOTERS

There have been over 2,000 books written about the Kennedy assassination and conspiracies that have mentioned many individuals as potential killers of the president. I asked the guide if he could give me the name of one of the shooters. His replied by giving me the initial:

H.

I followed up by inquiring if E. Howard Hunt had anything to do with the assassination and he answered:

YES.

E. Howard Hunt was a CIA officer from 1949 to 1970, who gained notoriety as one of the individuals who participated in the Watergate break-in that proved to be the downfall of President Nixon. Hunt was convicted of burglary, conspiracy, and wiretapping, eventually serving thirty-three months in prison. Even more importantly, before Hunt died in 2007, he made a deathbed confession that tied him to the JFK assassination. In his confession he implicated other individuals as well.

Next I asked the guide the name of an additional shooter and he gave me the initial:

S.

I inquired if any of the shooters ever went to jail and the answer was:

FRANK.

The identity of the shooter with the initial "S" was my next question. The guide replied:

STURGIS, GORDON.

The name Gordon did not ring a bell, so I asked if Gordon was a shooter. The mystery was solved when the guide replied:

SUPPOSED TO BE, LIDDY.

Sometimes I am a little slow so I said, Are you telling me that G. Gordon Liddy was involved in the conspiracy? His answer was:

SUPPOSED TO BE, YES.

When I asked what his involvement was the reply was:

BACKUP.

A Carcano Model 91/38 firing a 6.5 x 52 mm round.
Similar to rifle attributed to Oswald.

**Dallas Book Depository Building
showing the sixth-floor window and the roof
where the conspirator fired the killing shot.**
Courtesy Dollarphotoclub.

Was he involved with the Mafia? The guide replied:

No, CIA.

I guess the agency really was upset with the Kennedys! Gordon Liddy was the chief operative for the CIA that supervised the Watergate break-in. Liddy was convicted of burglary, conspiracy, and refusing to testify to the senate committee investigating Watergate. He served nearly fifty-two months in federal prisons. There was definitely a long-term relationship between Liddy and Howard Hunt. Keep in mind that the Bay of Pigs fiasco was also a CIA operation. As I mentioned earlier, the crackdown on organized crime was interfering with the drug running that provided funds for CIA black operations.

One of the Watergate break-in agents caught in the act by DC police was Frank Sturgis. Are the readers starting to see a pattern here? All three of the names given by the master guides worked together for the CIA and participated in the Watergate conspiracy that brought an end to the political career of Richard Nixon. Sturgis was sent to prison for his participation in the Watergate affair. In addition, Sturgis was one of the individuals named in Howard Hunt's deathbed confession.

The information for this chapter was collected over several channeling sessions with different guides. I asked another master guide if Howard Hunt played a role in the conspiracy. His answer was:

ONE ASSASSIN.

Next, I inquired if he actually fired a shot at the president and the answer was:

YES.

When I asked if he was on the grassy knoll when he fired the shot, the guide replied:

BEHIND.

My next question was behind what and the answer was:

FENCE.

At a later time during the interview with the spirit of the president, I asked JFK who was on the grassy knoll and he gave me the initial:

S.

I would take that to verify the presence of Frank Sturgis on the grassy knoll. I also asked him if Howard Hunt was involved and his answer was:

YES.

Witnesses indicated there were multiple individuals on the grassy knoll behind a fence at the time shots were fired. If you review the testimony of persons present in Dealy Plaza at the time of the shooting, forty of them told the police that the shots were fired from the knoll. The testimony by these witnesses was largely ignored by the various investigations, especially the Warren Commission. From the statements of the guides and the spirit of John Kennedy, I would assume that two of those individuals on the grassy knoll and behind the fence were Frank Sturgis and E. Howard Hunt.

THE MOTIVE AND CONSPIRATORS

I asked the master guide why Kennedy was assassinated and his reply was:

HE WAS TO BRING AN END TO THE VIETNAM WAR.

When I inquired who did not want the war to end, the answer was:

GOVERNMENTS, JOHNSON A MAJOR PLAYER.

The next obvious question asked if Lyndon Johnson was responsible for the murder of John Kennedy. I was not surprised to hear:

ONE AMONG OTHERS.

When I asked if he made the decision to go ahead with the assassination, the answer was:

YES.

The Kennedys had made many enemies and apparently several of them had gotten together to kill this most powerful man. I had always thought Cuba had played some role in the conspiracy, so I asked if Castro had retaliated for the Bay of Pigs invasion. I was surprised when the answer was:

NO, VIETNAM AND CIA DRUG RUNNING.

When I asked who was behind the assassination, the answer was:

YOUR GOVERNMENT.

Did the Secret Service know about the plan? The guide responded:

THEY WERE COMPLICIT.

I found it very hard to believe the agency assigned to protect the president cooperated in his assassination. When I asked if the Secret Service was warned before the shooting the guide said:

YES.

We were discovering that the conspiracy reached the highest levels of our government and even reached those sworn to protect the president. I had always heard that organized crime played a role in the conspiracy, so I asked if the

Mafia was involved, and the reply from the guide was:

YES.

Did organized crime get involved because of the pressure being brought by then Attorney General Bobby Kennedy? The reply was:

THAT AND THEY WERE HIRED GUNS.

I read in my research that Sam Giancana, the boss of the Chicago mob, was implicated in the assassination. When I inquired if he was in charge of the conspiracy for the Mafia the answer was:

YES.

I had read somewhere that Carlos Marcello, the head of the New Orleans crime family for over thirty years, was a mobster who was also somehow involved, so I asked the guide? His answer was:

TRAFFICKING AND THE ARCHITECT.

THE SPIRIT OF THE PRESIDENT SPEAKS

The previous paragraphs gave details of the reasons for the assassination and the conspirators in the words of the heavenly guides. One evening during a channeling session I asked for the spirit of John Kennedy to appear to us so I could verify the information from the individual who had lived the events.

The interview with the spirit of Jack Kennedy was a humbling experience. Barbara Lee and I had been selected to be the recipients of historic information that had eluded researchers and investigative authors for over fifty years. I was struck by the modest nature of the president. When he first recorded his presence into our session he signed in as:

JACK.

When I asked if I should address him as Mr. President, the said:

THAT WILL NOT BE NECESSARY.

When I asked the same questions of the spirit of the president, the answers were pretty much the same as well, but he added more details. I started out by inquiring if he intended to remove the troops from Vietnam, and he replied:

YES.

Next, I asked if the removal of troops was the main reason for his murder. His answer was:

ONE REASON.

When I asked the main reason he quickly spelled out:

MAFIA.

I had never realized that organized crime in our country was so powerful they could succeed in killing the president! My follow-up question was: Are you saying your cracking down on organized crime was the main reason for the taking of your life? JFK replied:

YES, AND MY FATHER.

Joseph Kennedy amassed a fortune during and after prohibition in the alcohol industry. He also owned the largest office building in the country, the Chicago Merchandise Mart. My guess is that Joseph Kennedy must have had some problems with the mob in his past dealings. I then asked the same question that had been put to the master guide in earlier sessions: Who was the head of the Mafia that ordered your murder? His answer was the same as that of the guide:

GIANCANA.

Apparently, the mob was the mastermind behind the assassination, but they had a lot of other help within our government.

The guides all said that Vice President Johnson was one of the driving forces behind the killing, so I asked if Lyndon Johnson was involved. No one in the room was surprised when the answer was:

YES.

I asked JFK if it was because Johnson wanted to become President? He replied:

PART OF THE PLAN, JOHNSON ALSO HIRED GUNS.

I now inquired if the Secret Service aided in the murder plan and the answer was:

THEY DID.

I asked the question: Who do you blame most for the assassination? The answer was:

JOHNSON, HE GAVE THE ORDERS.

One final question about LBJ: I inquired if he was the individual who got the Mafia involved and the answer was:

YES.

My guess is that after Johnson left the presidency, he had an awful lot on his conscience to live with.

THE AFTERMATH

Immediately after the shooting, a Dallas policeman named J. C. Tippet was shot four times near Dealy Plaza. The official story is that officer Tippett spotted Oswald on the street and was shot while attempting to apprehend him. For fifty years the conspiracy theorists have tried to fill in the details of why Officer Tippett was so far from his normal locations. At the time of the policeman's murder, a description of Oswald had been broadcast over police radio. One theory is that he was part of the conspiracy and his role was to provide a means for Oswald to escape the area. Another theory states that he was killed to provide a reason to pick up Oswald.

I asked the guides who killed J. D. Tippet, and the reply was:

MAFIA HIT.

When I re-asked if the Mafia was involved the answer was:

YES.

My next question inquired why the officer was killed by the Mafia, and the answer was:

TURNED.

I followed up by asking if he was part of the conspiracy and turned on the assassins, and the answer was:

YES.

Judging from the answers, I believe that Officer Tippett was part of the conspiracy but did not follow through with his role and received four bullets for turning on the mobsters. I would like to propose that Officer Tippett was supposed to kill Oswald—the old "dead men tell no tales" thing. When he did not kill Oswald, the policeman was in turn executed for crossing the Mafia.

After the shooting of Officer Tippett, Oswald was arrested by Dallas Police in a movie theatre. His time in captivity was very short, but when questioned, he said he was having lunch during the shooting and was being framed for the murder. The next day, he was killed by Jack Ruby, the owner of a Dallas strip club, in the police station while surrounded by security. Jack Ruby was originally from Chicago where he was said to have connections with Sam Giancana. I would remind the reader that according to the guides, Sam Giacana was the Mafia boss in charge of the assassination.

Jack Ruby was convicted for the killing of Oswald but was ordered to have a new trial. Before the new trial, he died of a pulmonary embolism as a result of very aggressive lung cancer. Ironically, he died at Parkland Hospital, the same place that Kennedy was pronounced dead. Before he passed, Ruby told a deputy sheriff that they had injected him for a cold, but he felt it was cancer cells. I asked the guides who hired Jack Ruby and the answer was:

Jack Ruby kills Oswald while in Police custody.
Courtesy US Archives.

Intelligence.

When I asked how they got him to kill Oswald the reply was:

Threat.

For someone to be coerced into killing such a high-profile individual there had to be a very serious threat. Did they threaten his family? The answer was:

Death.

Before he was diagnosed with cancer, Ruby conducted an in-depth interview with Dorothy Kilgallen a famous columnist for the *New York Journal*. Aware that other journalists involved in the investigation had severe physical problems, she handed a copy of the interview notes to a friend, Margaret Smith. Shortly after the interview and before she could report the results of her conversations with Ruby, she died of mysterious causes. She reportedly had told a few friends after her Ruby interview that she was "about to blow the JFK case sky high." The results of her autopsy were listed as "circumstances undetermined." Her friend Margaret Smith died two days after Kilgallen. I asked the guides if

Dorothy Kilgallen was killed and the reply was:

LATER IN TIME.

When I inquired what she learned during the interview with Jack Ruby, the reply was:

HE WAS AFRAID FOR HIS LIFE.

He obviously had good reason to fear for his life. The conspirators even had journalists killed who threatened their dirty little secrets. I asked the guides how many witnesses to the assassination were killed and the answer was:

3 TO BE CERTAIN.

The body of the fallen president was removed to Bethesda Naval Hospital for the autopsy in spite of the fact that Texas law required the autopsy to be performed in the Lone Star State. Autopsy photographs made public at the time indicated that the first bullet hit at the base of the neck and exited the throat. A second bullet hit the President in the right side of the head and exploded parts of his skull. I asked the guide if his autopsy photographs were altered. His answer was:

ALL WAS COVERED.

My follow-up question was if the autopsy photos in the National Archives were actually those of JFK. In response he replied:

ACTUAL PHOTOS ARE CONCEALED.

On November 29, 1963, a commission was established by President Lyndon Johnson to investigate the killing of President Kennedy. In retrospect, this is one of the best examples of all time of the fox watching the hen house. The group of appointees was known as the Warren Commission after Chief Justice Earl Warren. Gerald Ford, a member of the Commission, was House minority leader at the time and would go on to become president. The findings of the commission declared that Oswald was the killer and single shooter. When I asked the guide if the findings of the Warren Commission were manipulated, the answer was:

YES.

I was not surprised by that answer by the guide. Roger Stone was an assistant to Richard Nixon and author of *The Man Who Killed Kennedy: The Case Against LBJ*. Stone said Nixon described the Warren Commission as "the greatest hoax ever perpetrated," telling him, "The difference between LBJ and me was we both wanted to be president, but I wouldn't kill for it." Nixon apparently knew what happened but was unwilling to take a chance on doing anything about it. I can't say that I blame him.

LYNDON JOHNSON AND FORGIVENESS

As the interview with President Kennedy progressed, I thought I would ask him some questions about the person who ordered his execution and their relationship on the other side. Have you ever seen Lyndon Johnson on the other side? I asked. From other interviews I had grown to believe spirits avoid the spirits responsible for their deaths. His answer surprised me, it was:

I HAVE.

I followed up by asking, Has he apologized for having you killed? The answer was not exactly what I was expecting. He replied:

YES, HE KILLED HIMSELF.

It took a little while to recover from that answer. Are you saying Lyndon Johnson committed suicide?

YES, HE DID.

How did he do it? JFK answered:

GUNSHOT. COVERED UP.

In all my research, I had never read any report that LBJ had committed suicide, so I inquired as to how they covered it up. The reply was:

HEART.

Are you saying he shot himself in the heart? Kennedy replied:

NO, HEAD.

My guess is our honored guest was losing respect for his interviewer. He obviously meant that they covered up the suicide of Lyndon Johnson by saying he had a heart attack. I then asked if he had forgiven the man who had planned and executed his death and the answer was:

YES.

Forgiveness is a wonderful thing. I thought I would ask the spirit of the president about some other conspiracies that centered on the Kennedy family. My first questions involved the killing of his brother, Bobby Kennedy, who was shot while beginning a run for President.

Lyndon Johnson,
the chief conspirator.

THE KILLING OF BOBBY KENNEDY

In 1965, Bobby Kennedy was elected to the United States Senate from the state of New York. Lyndon Johnson announced he would not seek re-election in 1968 amid growing unrest over the escalation of the War in Vietnam. Bobby Kennedy entered the Presidential race and had won primaries in the states of California and South Dakota and appeared to be a very strong candidate. While attending a function after the California primary, a Palestinian Arab with Jordanian citizenship and strong anti-Zionist views assassinated Bobby Kennedy with a small-caliber pistol. Sirhan Sirhan was convicted and is still serving a life term in a California jail.

During our session with the master guide, I asked him if the Mafia was responsible for the killing of Robert Kennedy. His reply was:

YES, AND THE CIA.

In the later interview with the spirit of JFK, I asked if Bobby was killed by the same people who had him killed. The spirit of the president answered:

SAME GROUP.

Apparently, the unholy alliance of Johnson and the Mafia had no intention of allowing a Kennedy back in the office of president of the United States.

Robert F. Kennedy, brother of Jack Kennedy.
Courtesy US Archives.

THE DEATH OF JOHN KENNEDY JR.

As I discussed earlier in this chapter, on July 16, 1999, John Kennedy Jr., along with his wife and sister-in-law, were killed while flying in a light aircraft off the coast of Martha's Vineyard. He was not an inexperienced pilot. At the time of the crash he had flown a total of 310 hours with 55 of them being at night. He had taken the written exam for instrument certification but needed additional training time with an instructor. Visibility at the time was ten miles, diminishing to four miles in the vicinity of Martha's Vineyard. There was never a distress call, and all passengers were killed on impact.

During a session last year, we were channeling with the spirit of Buddy Holly. For those of you not old enough to remember, in 1959, he was killed in the crash of a small plane with many of the most famous stars of early rock and roll. Don McLean wrote the song "American Pie," with the famous lyric "the day the music died," after the death of the musical celebrities. The purpose of the appearance of Buddy Holly was to tell us that his plane crash was no accident. He blamed it on the actions of the Mafia attempting to muscle into the music industry. At the end of the session, he said that the same thing happened to John Kennedy Jr. Needless to say, I was anxious to pursue the event with the guides and JFK Sr.

During one of our channeling sessions I asked the guide if John Kennedy Jr. was assassinated and the reply was:

Yes.

I then asked who was behind the plan to kill the younger Kennedy, and the answer was:

Government.

It seems like we have been hearing that answer a lot lately! Our group had been told that the reason for his death was that he was going to reopen the investigation into his father's assassination. The guide verified the reason by answering:

Yes.

I then inquired if the truth would ever come out and he replied:

Yes.

When asked about when the information would become public, he replied:

Decades.

At least there is hope there will be justice at some time in the future. During the interview with JFK Sr., I inquired if his son was killed. As I expected, he said:

Yes.

My next question was why they killed John Jr., and the answer was:

He was going to name names.

It is quite unnerving to know there are still corrupt people in our government capable of killing our citizens to protect the names of the Kennedy conspirators. My final question on this subject was if his son was with him on the other side, and his reply was:

Yes.

At least their souls are together on the other side.

BAY OF PIGS AND THE
CUBAN MISSILE CRISIS

Even though the Bay of Pigs invasion did not seem to play a role in the assassination other than strongly irritating the CIA, I thought I would attempt to find out what really took place. I started by asking if he had approved the order that deprived the ground assault of air support. His answer was:

IT WAS ARRANGED WITHOUT MY KNOWLEDGE.

When I inquired why the decision was made, JFK replied:

TIES TO CUBA OF SOME.

Who had ties to Cuba? His reply was:

JOHNSON, MAFIA, CIA.

Sounds like the same group that arranged for the conspiracy! When asked if the Bay of Pigs fiasco was a deliberate attempt to make him look bad politically, the answer was:

YES.

When the aerial photographs indicated the presence of missiles capable of delivering nuclear warheads, the joint chiefs of staff wanted to bomb the sites, destroying the missiles and killing the Soviet technicians. Kennedy overruled the military and decided to do a naval blockade of Cuba instead. I asked if he was really prepared to wage nuclear war because of the crisis. He replied:

I TALKED ABOUT IT BUT COULD NOT.

If the Soviets had refused to remove the missiles, would you have conducted an air raid and destroyed the site in Cuba? To that question the answer was:

YES.

I finished by asking if we were really at risk of nuclear war and the president replied:

NOT SURE.

The threat of the Cuban missile crisis was real and not even President Kennedy knew for certain the eventual outcome. Nikita Khrushchev was the chairman of the Soviet Union at the time of the missile crisis. The Russians had just scored a victory by putting the first man in space, while Kennedy had suffered a defeat at the Bay of Pigs. The world knew relatively little about the Soviet leader except that he was short, heavyset, wore suits that did not fit, and had public fits of rage. I asked JFK his opinion of Krushchev and his answer was:

Ugh.

I took that not to be a compliment. When I asked if he ever saw him on the other side he replied:

No.

Spirits can definitely pick who they associate with on the other side.

Nikita Khrushchev,
Chairman of the Soviet Union, and President Kennedy.
Courtesy US Archives.

LIFE ON THE OTHER SIDE OF THE VEIL

During our interview, I asked him what it was like to be over there. His answer was:

PEACE.

It was good to know that the victim of such a violent end, at the peak of his career, was at rest and had found peace. When I questioned him whether there were any other spirits in the room on that evening, the reply was:

NO.

From our experience with communicating with the other side, I knew there was a series of realms, and as the soul moves on, it advances to higher ones. Evil individuals reside in the lower realms. When I realized he was not with other spirits, I asked if he was in a different realm. JFK answered:

YES, I'VE MOVED ON.

Once a soul moves on, it is possible for it to return to the lower realms. We have been told many times that the soul makes the decision if it is going to reincarnate. My next question was if his soul was going to reincarnate again. His answer was:

NO.

Are you telling me that you have had enough on the side of the life veil? JFK answered:

QUITE.

The soul of the thirty-fifth president had enough of the evil and brutality that took his life, that of his brother, and his son's. I certainly can't blame him for wanting the peace found in the heavenly realms rather than the turmoil of life on this side. We have been told many times by the guides that the purpose of reincarnation is soul experiences and learning lessons. I asked President Kennedy the main life lesson learned during his incarnate visit. His reply caught me off guard:

THE LESSON WAS MY FATHER'S.

As I stated earlier, Joseph Kennedy was an extremely powerful man that often twisted the laws to his advantage. When I heard the reply, I was unclear as to its meaning. I asked JFK if his father was with him on the other side. His reply was:

NOT NOW. MY FATHER WAS NOT A GOOD MAN.

I followed up by inquiring where he is now; to which he replied:

Not here.

I already knew the answer, but asked if there was a different place for evil. The president answered:

Yes, low.

He just confirmed that the lower realm is reserved for the evil. A life of wealth and power abused can get you in a very nasty place on the other side.

OTHER SECRETS, OBAMA, MARILYN, AND TED

President Kennedy was a moderate Democrat that in many ways pursued conservative policies, such as lower taxes to stimulate business. His assassination was the result of him trying to do what was right for the citizens of the country. I decided to throw caution to the wind and ask him what he thought of our current president. His answer was:

Not good!

My next inquiry was more of a statement than a question: The current political party is not like your Democratic party. The answer was:

Not at all.

Has he messed up your Democratic party was my next question, and he answered:

He has.

Now I inquired if he had any current concerns over what is happening today, and JFK responded:

All is much changed. Will never be the same.

I fear he is correct. Since spirits get around a lot, I asked the past president if he ever visits the White House. He replied:

Yes, visit.

I got the impression he did not spend a lot of time there. I made a very special request: The next time you go, will you kick Obama in the butt for me? I could almost see the smile on the spirit's face as he said:

With pleasure.

After a slight hesitation, he gave us the message:

I PRAY FOR THE WORLD.

In spite of all the time I spent communicating with spirits in the afterlife, I did not realize the spirits still prayed on the other side.

I figured that I would clear up a few more loose ends. Jack Kennedy was a man who cared deeply for his country but had clay feet. I took a deep breath and asked him if he had ever slept with Marilyn Monroe. His reply was:

I DID.

While we were on touchy subjects, I asked if his brother, Ted, could have saved the life of Mary Jo Kopechne in the car accident at Chappaquiddick Island in 1969. The spirit of the past president answered:

YES, I AM DISAPPOINTED IN HIM. HE WAS SET UP BUT COULD HAVE SAVED THE GIRL.

We were coming to the end of my questions, so I asked if he had anything else that he wanted published. He answered:

I KNEW IT WAS COMING.

Jack and Jackie Kennedy in Dallas in the open vehicle.
Courtesy US Archives.

How did you know? His reply was:

HUNCH.

I guess if you've irritated the Mafia, joint chiefs of staff, CIA, Cuba, Cuban Nationals, and Russia, there might be enough reasons to have a hunch something bad was going to happen. I asked why he took the chance of riding in an open car. He answered:

I WAS NO COWARD.

Jack Kennedy was certainly no coward. His exploits during WWII in the Navy had won him well-deserved medals. When a Jap destroyer cut his PT boat in half, he swam miles, saving the lives of his men. When I told him how impressed I was with his incredible war record, he answered:

THANK YOU.

I told him that God had saved him for greater things. In response he replied:

HE DID, BUT OTHERS PREVENTED IT.

The spirit of the thirty-fifth president of the United States was quite modest in spite of his accomplishments. When I asked him if he had any more messages, the answer was:

NOT AT THIS TIME.

I thanked him for speaking with us and the last message we received was:

GOD BLESS AND THANK YOU.

This was the spirit of a truly great individual. If any of you have doubts as to the accuracy of the context of this chapter, I have actual video and audio recordings on file that verify every word in this chapter. Perhaps the best exchange with JFK took place when I asked him if he would be willing to visit with us again in the future and he replied:

IF IT CAN BE ARRANGED.

I look forward to communicating one more time with this great American hero. It is indeed regrettable that his spirit has decided not to reincarnate. We could surely use him today. ∞

CHAPTER 14

BUTCH CASSIDY AND THE SUNDANCE KID

OUTSMARTING THE LAW

The name Butch Cassidy became a household name in 1969 when Paul Newman and Robert Redford starred in the movie *Butch Cassidy and the Sundance Kid*. Newman and Redford played the leaders of the notorious Hole-in-the-Wall gang that robbed banks and trains in the late 1800s. They glamorized the two outlaws to the point where you felt sorry for them when they died in Bolivia, the country they'd fled to in order not to be arrested by the famous Pinkerton Detectives. I never thought too much about their demise until watching a show on the American Heroes Channel that insinuated they did not die in Bolivia as advertised. While watching the program, I realized their story would make a great chapter for this book.

A GOOD MORMON FAMILY

Born with the non-outlaw name Robert LeRoy Parker in April of 1866 to Mormon parents in Beaver, Utah, the man who came to be known as Butch Cassidy was the oldest of thirteen children. Robert Parker moved from the family home at an early age in an attempt to fend for himself. He took a job with a local rancher/rustler named Mike Cassidy. By 1884, he was participating in cattle rustling under the guidance of his new employer, who taught him to ride and shoot. Not wanting his new occupation to reflect upon his family, he took the name of Cassidy to honor his new boss. His life as an outlaw took shape while in his early teens. His first major event outside the law took place in 1889, when Cassidy and a group of his friends robbed the San Miguel Valley Bank in Telluride, Colorado, of more than $20,000.

Shortly after robbing the bank, he moved to Rock Springs, Wyoming, and worked in a butcher shop. It is believed that during this time he took the name Butch, a shortened version of butcher. While working in Wyoming in 1894, he was framed for stealing a horse worth $5 and sentenced to two years in the state penitentiary. As the story goes, he was released after eighteen months after promising the governor that he would not steal from the Wyoming ranchers in the future. Having no intention of going straight, he became associated with a group of outlaws called the Wild Bunch. It wasn't long until the group went

Butch Cassidy mug shot, Wyoming State Prison.
Courtesy Wyoming State Archives.

from stealing horses to robbing trains and banks. He did keep his word and stayed out of Wyoming.

Butch Cassidy, probably one of the most intelligent of the western outlaws, was known for detailed planning of his robberies. He would spend days scouting the locations and have elaborate escape plans. One of his favorite plans would involve having fresh horses planted along the escape route so they could outride a pursuing posse. He and his gang were quite active carrying out robberies throughout the 1890s but were not known to be violent. During the events he would actually be quite polite and is believed to have never personally killed anyone.

Harry Alonzo Longabaugh, born in Pennsylvania, became a member of the Wild Bunch. He was given the name Sundance Kid because he served eighteen months in the Sundance Prison in Wyoming for stealing horses.

He was released in 1889 and became a friend of Butch Cassidy. For the next ten years the fame of the outlaws grew, attracting the wrath of the railroads and embarrassed lawmen.

A STUPID PICTURE

In September 1900, Cassidy, the Kid, and another gang member named Bill Carver robbed a bank in Winnemucca, Nevada, of almost $33,000. From there the gang went to Fort Worth, Texas, where, while partying with the local women, they made their first major mistake: they posed for a group photograph.

Butch Cassidy and the Wild Bunch.
Front row left to right: Harry A. Longabaugh, alias the Sundance Kid; Ben Kilpatrick, alias the Tall Texan; Robert Leroy Parker, alias Butch Cassidy. Standing: Will Carver, alias News Carver; and Harvey Logan, alias Kid Curry. Fort Worth, Texas, 1900. Public Domain.

Pinkerton Detectives obtained a copy of the photograph, and for the first time had detailed pictures of the individuals whose identities up to this time could not be discovered. The Wild Bunch now saw their faces widely distributed on wanted posters. In July 1901, the gang robbed the Great Northern Railroad of over $60,000. In case you are interested, that equates to $1.7 million in current purchasing power. This was the straw that broke the proverbial camel's back. The railroads gave the Pinkertons orders to chase down the Wild Bunch and stop them from making cash withdrawals from their trains. After the Great Northern robbery, the gang separated.

TIME TO HEAD TO SOUTH AMERICA

Cassidy and the Sundance Kid made their way to New York City. In February 1902, they boarded the British steamer, *Herminius*, and headed for Buenos Aires, Argentina. They eventually purchased a 15,000-acre ranch near Cholila, Argentina, and settled down to raise cattle. Everything would have worked out well for Cassidy and the Kid except for one little thing. Apparently, they could not stop robbing trains. The railroads sent the Pinkerton Detectives to Argentina to chase down the pair. Cassidy got word of the approach of the detectives and, in May 1905, sold the ranch and took off before their arrival.

Now here is where the facts become a little shaky. It is known that Cassidy worked for a while at the Concordia Tin Mine in the central Bolivian Andes and that he was joined by Longabaugh at that location. In late 1907, the pair traveled to the town of Santa Cruz on the Bolivian frontier, and nothing is known about their whereabouts for a period of time as they'd dropped out of sight.

According to the history books, almost a year later in southern Bolivia, a courier for a silver mining company was held up by two English-speaking masked bandits. It was assumed the crooks were Butch Cassidy and the Sundance Kid. The robbers went to a small mining town named San Vincente and rented a room. They had a mule in their possession that bore the brand of the mining company that had just been held up. The owner of the boarding house notified the Bolivian Army that dispatched cavalry to investigate if it was indeed the robbers of the silver mine. A gunfight broke out, and the two robbers were driven into a building surrounded by the Bolivian cavalry and townspeople who had taken up arms. Apparently, the robbers were down to their last two bullets, which they used on each other. The bodies were buried in the town with no positive identification. It was assumed by most that Butch Cassidy and the Sundance Kid had met their end in a little town in Bolivia. The idea was confirmed in the famous 1969 movie.

NOT EVERYONE WAS CONVINCED

When William A. Pinkerton heard the news that the pair had been killed in a shoot-out at San Vincente, he believed the famous outlaws had once again found a way to throw the detectives off their trail, and stated: "The whole story is a fake." After the shoot-out, there were alleged sightings of the pair throughout Latin America. The Pinkerton Detective Agency never officially called off their hunt for Butch Cassidy and the Sundance Kid.

Whoever was killed in San Vincente were supposedly buried in an unmarked grave. In 1991, a forensic team from the United States dug up the grave that supposedly held the outlaws. DNA tests were run and the remains proved to be the body of a German Engineer, Gustave Zimmer, who worked at the local mines. The team was never able to find any remains that would resemble the pair.

Books and articles have been written both proving and disproving that Butch Cassidy and the Sundance Kid met their demise in Bolivia in 1908. There are equally strong arguments on both sides. After reading the arguments on both sides, I decided it was time to ask our spirit guides.

TIME TO ASK A GUIDE

I figured that it would be nice to know if I was wasting my time doing a chapter on Butch Cassidy, so one night when we were channeling, I asked Raz, our master guide, if Butch Cassidy died in Bolivia in 1908. He replied:

NO.

In an effort to verify the information, I inquired what year he really passed. His answer was right on track with rumors that he lived into old age:

1937.

What happened in Bolivia in 1908 where he and the Sundance Kid were supposed to have been killed in a shootout?

STAGED.

As mentioned, Cassidy was known for his detailed planning of his robberies. Staging his demise would certainly be within his capabilities. It did not make sense that he would undertake such a small robbery as the mine payroll when he had just sold his huge ranch in Argentina. It is also difficult to believe that he would have kept a mule with the brand of the mine he'd just robbed. My guess is he used some of his funds to hire the locals and cavalry to put on a show. With this initial information we ended the session with Raz, but I decided to attempt to talk to the soul of the famous outlaw in person.

CALL ME LEROY

A couple of weeks later, Connie and I were on the channeling board with the intent of contacting the famous outlaw. We were communicating with our usual dependable guide, Raz. I asked him if it would be possible to talk to the soul of Robert LeRoy Parker, better known as Butch Cassidy. The glass went to rest, meaning to wait a minute before continuing. Somehow there is this paging system on the other side and the "rest" statement usually means that our guide is tracking down the desired spirit. This time was no exception and when, after a short delay, I asked again if the spirit of LeRoy Parker was present, the answer was:

Yes.

We always attempt to verify that we are indeed in contact with the right spirit, so I asked him for information that the average spirit would not be aware of. My first question inquired what year he passed.

1936.

That was one year off from the date I found in my research and what Raz had told me earlier, but I would think the spirit himself would be the best judge of when he died. It certainly wasn't the 1908 in the history books. My follow-up question asked where he passed.

WA.

All indications were that he really died in the state of Washington. We were indeed in the presence of Robert LeRoy Parker, a.k.a. Butch Cassidy. Whenever we are introduced to a spirit for the first time I usually ask how they would like me to refer to them. I asked if he would like me to call him Butch. He replied:

No.

Would you like me to call you LeRoy?

Yes.

Next, I made sure it was okay to inquire into the details of his life. Is it okay if I ask you some questions for the book I am writing on conspiracies?

Yes.

He was certainly coming across as a nice guy, just like they talked about him in the history books and in the movie. I thought I would start out by confirming what Raz had told me earlier. Did you stage your death in Bolivia?

Yes.

Are there any fake graves in Bolivia?

Yes.

When I asked if there were any bodies in those graves, he replied:

No.

So there was good reason the Pinkerton Detective Agency never closed the case and continued to search for the outlaw! He really had staged his death to throw off the police. He and Sundance had been living peacefully on their ranch in Argentina before winding up in Bolivia. It was reported that his activities in Argentina attracted the attention of the Pinkertons. I asked if he ever conducted any robberies in Argentina. He replied:

Yes.

My guess was he just could not resist his old habits. Next, I asked if he ever killed anyone. The glass went very rapid and forcibly to:

No.

He was quite proud that, in spite of all the robberies he was involved in, he never was forced to take the life of another human. I guess that is why he is not in one of the lower realms where I could not have contacted him. It was said that in 1925 he returned to Utah to visit his sister and let her know he was still alive. When I asked the question, he replied:

YES.

His family kept the secret until he passed in the 1930s. It was rumored that some of the money he stole is still hidden today, and that late in his life he attempted to search for it but could not find the cache. Next, I asked if indeed there was some of his money that was never found. His answer was:

YES.

Where is the lost money located?

UT.

Do you remember where it is located?

No.

So there really is hidden treasure in the wilds of the state of Utah. The 1969 movie made Butch Cassidy and the Sundance Kid famous. I asked him what he thought about the movie and he answered:

REAL.

But the ending was not correct.

No.

I ended the session by asking him if he was planning to reincarnate to which he said:

No.

I guess LeRoy is afraid that if his soul returns, Karma might catch up with him, and the Pinkertons might still find him. Robert LeRoy Parker was truly one of the great characters of the old west, and we were honored to interview him. His story deserves to be told as one of the great conspiracies in the early history of our country. ∞

MISCELLANEOUS MYSTERIES

AND DISAPPEARANCES

When I started to write this book I had no idea how many conspiracies and historical mysteries there were to research. After working on it for two years, I have come to the conclusion that it was time to stop writing and send it to the publisher. In this final chapter I am going to do the equivalent of a lightning round and give some short answers to multiple mysteries and disappearances that have not been addressed elsewhere.

ILLUMINATI AND THE NEW WORLD ORDER

The word "Illuminati" literally means "one who is illuminated" or "the enlightened ones." Historically, Adam Weiskaupt founded the Order of the Illuminati on May 1, 1776, in Bavaria. Today it is rumored that its members have formed a society of the richest and most powerful individuals in order to form a New World Order. Their society is believed to have permeated all layers of our culture, including prominent Christians. It has been stated that the main deterrent to taking over our country is the Second Amendment, our right to bear arms. I read one article that suggested that as many as one percent of the population of our country are Illuminati members.

One evening in October 2013, I asked the master guide if the Illuminati currently exists as a secret society. Unfortunately for us, his reply was:

YES.

It is my understanding that most of the richest families in the world are members. I started by asking if the Rockefellers were members.

YES.

The Kennedys?

YES.

George W. Bush?

YES.

Stars in Hollywood?

YES.

I could see where this was going. Political parties make no difference, it is the people with money, the ability to influence people, and power. I thought I would change the questioning to government institutions. Our Federal Reserve has a huge effect on not only our financial matters but those of the world. I inquired if the Illuminati controlled the Federal Reserve. The reply by the master guide was even more disturbing.

THEY CONTROL GOVERNMENT.

The answer implied they have control over almost everything in Washington, DC. If they control the Federal Reserve, they have an unbelievable control over our economy. I asked if it was their intent to bring the global economy to its knees.

IN TIME WILL ATTEMPT TO.

In recent times we have seen that our scholastic ratings, when compared with other countries, have been decreasing. When I inquired if the dumbing down of our public schools was part of the New World Order plan. The reply was:

YES.

Current events in the Middle East are quite troubling with ISIS controlling large areas and the greatest humanitarian crisis taking place since WWII. My next question was: Are the Illuminati planning WWIII to pit the West against Islam?"

IT IS ALREADY WRITTEN.

Will WWIII soon begin?

WITHIN A DECADE. ONCE ISRAEL IS INVOLVED, YOU WILL KNOW IT HAS BEGUN.

There wasn't a lot of good news in those messages. I inquired: With everything that is happening, is there any way for good to prevail?

GOOD ALWAYS PREVAILS.

At least we ended the session on a note of optimism.

WORLD TRADE CENTER ATTACK

Our world changed on September 11, 2001, when Al Qaeda members flew passenger planes into the two towers of the World Trade Center and the Pentagon. Many conspiracy theorists say that our federal government was behind the bombings. While I believe the federal government is behind a lot of unsavory projects, I never believed 9/11 was one of them. I asked the question directly whether our government was involved with the Twin Tower bombings.

THEY WERE FOREWARNED THAT SOMETHING MAJOR WOULD OCCUR.

Were they part of the plan?

NO.

I had heard that they believed something big was in the works but did not have enough details to stop the attack. I asked if they intentionally ignored the warnings.

NO.

If you remember, prior to 9/11 many of our security agencies did a poor job of communicating. For all we know, they may still have the same problem. Our government received advance warning of some type of attack, but details were lacking. Hopefully, it will never happen again, but according to the guides, very bad things are being planned.

WEAPONS OF MASS DESTRUCTION IN IRAQ

The Country of Iraq held many types of weapons of mass destruction prior to the First Iraq War. They had used biological weapons on the Kurds and conducted one of the most secretive weapons programs in history. The United Nations sent in inspection teams, but they were refused access to important areas. When the teams were expelled from the country, NATO had to rely on intelligence sources that corroborated the existence of the weapons. By March 2003, the allies were convinced that Iraq possessed weapons of mass destruction and began the Second Gulf War.

As the war progressed, no weapons of mass destruction were located within the country of Iraq, and anti-war sentiment took over the allied countries. I had always wondered if Iraq had simply moved the weapons to a different location. One evening I thought I would ask our guide what really happened in Iraq. I started by asking if at the time of the Second Gulf War, Iraq had weapons of mass destruction. His answer was direct and to the point:

YES.

Did the United States use the weapons of mass destruction as an excuse to invade the country?

NO, THEY WERE PRESENT AT THAT TIME.

Where were they shipped?

Turkey.

Turkey is supposed to be an ally and a NATO member. Did the United States know the weapons were moved?

Yes.

The guide confirmed that WMDs were present at the time of the attack of the Second Gulf War. They were moved to the country of our so-called ally, Turkey. We are definitely living in a time that you never know who you can trust, including our own government. Maybe we shouldn't be quite as hard on George W. Bush and his allies. According to the guides, the Iraqis were just a little too quick in hiding the weapons.

THE KNIGHTS TEMPLAR, THE HOLY GRAIL, AND THE ARK OF THE COVENANT

We have all heard of the Holy Grail. We were told by the guides it was a document that described the secret teachings of Jesus to his Apostles. Our Lord thought that the general public was not as yet ready for these secret teachings.

One evening we were channeling with Pope Sylvester 1st, the pope in 325 AD during the time of the First Council of Nicaea, when Constantine selected the books of the Bible. I told the Pope I understood that many gospels were omitted:

There were many gospels missing.

Did Constantine discuss with you what books would be included?

I was conferred with.

Why were some of the books left out?

I was not in agreement with all.

Which books were left out?

Teachings of Jesus.

The Holy Grail, the secret teachings of Jesus, were deliberately omitted from the gospels selected for the Bible. I asked if the secret teachings could be recovered today?

Not entirely.

Why were they left out?

THERE WERE FEARS.

Did the secret teachings of Jesus include discussions of extraterrestrials?

HE SPOKE OF THEM, YES.

How did Jesus refer to the aliens?

OTHER BEINGS.

Did Jesus include reincarnation in his secret teachings?

YES.

Emperor Constantine was attempting to solidify his political power by bringing Christians out of the shadows. Accuracy of the gospels were not his chief priority. I asked if Constantine made the final decisions on what books were to be removed:

YES.

The most important part of the gospels, the Holy Grail, the secret teachings of Jesus were omitted from the bible, but what happened to the written documents? I asked the guide if the Knights Templar were given possession of the Holy Grail?

ARK OF THE COVENANT.

The Ark of the Covenant is the container that is thought to hold the tablets of stone upon which are written the Ten Commandments. The guide had just told me the Ark of the Covenant was entrusted to the Knights Templar. I asked if the Ark still exists?

YES.

There are many rumors about the control of the Ark of the Covenant. I asked if the Illuminati, the powerful secret socialist organization, controlled the Ark. The guide answered:

NO.

There was a rumor Columbus brought the Ark of the Covenant to the New World. When I asked the question, the guide said:

NO.

I asked who controlled it, and the answer was:

SECRET.

I can guarantee you the secret of who controls the Ark of the Covenant is secure in the hand of the spirit guides!

DISAPPEARANCE OF THE CREW OF THE
MARY CELESTE

One of the most famous of all maritime disappearances happened in 1872 when a merchant brigantine, the *Mary Celeste*, was found floating and intact off the Azores Islands. On November 15, the ship left the New York harbor headed for Genoa, Italy. The ship carried a cargo of 1,700 barrels of industrial alcohol and a crew of seven plus Captain Benjamin Briggs, his wife, and two-year-old daughter. Briggs was a highly talented captain, and his crew was carefully selected for the voyage. On December 5, the vessel was found with the cargo intact, the lifeboat missing, and six months of food on board the boat, floating between the Azores and the coast of Portugal. All ten individuals on board were missing without a trace.

One evening, in 2015, I asked Mou, our alien guide, what happened to the passengers and crew of the *Mary Celeste*. His answer only added to the mystery.

THEY WERE NEEDED.

In an effort to clarify what we had just been told, I inquired why they were needed.

TO LEARN ABOUT THEIR MASTERY OF CELESTIAL NAVIGATION.

I could see where this conversation was headed and asked the obvious: Are you saying they were abducted by aliens?

YES.

What happened after they were abducted?

IT WENT WRONG.

Are you saying they died as a result of the abduction? There was no answer to that question so I rephrased the question. Were they killed?

NO, BUT THEY DIED.

This was the first time I'd heard that the victims died as a result of an abduction. My guess is that the rules for abductions in the nineteenth century were far different from today. I asked what they did to the bodies.

VAPORIZED.

I guess that explains why the bodies were never found. If you read my book on aliens, you realize that I have been told before aliens cover their mistakes. According to our guide, the *Mary Celeste* crew suffered from an alien abduction gone bad.

WHAT HAPPENED TO AMELIA EARHART?

Amelia Earhart was the most famous female aviator of her time. She gained fame by being the first woman to fly solo across the Atlantic Ocean. In addition to her flying feats, she was a best-selling author and a political activist as well as an early supporter of the Equal Rights Amendment. In 1937, she attempted to circumnavigate the globe in a Lockheed Model 10 Electra specially modified for the flight. The Electra was equipped with a radio directional system intended to provide navigational capabilities. Various radio contacts with Earhart indicated confusion and an inability to locate her true position. The plane disappeared without a trace near Howland Island in the central Pacific Ocean. Her disappearance remains a mystery to this day. There were even rumors that the Japanese had shot down her plane.

I thought I would attempt to solve this long-standing mystery during one of our channeling sessions. My first question was direct and to the point. "What happened to Amelia Earhart?"

INTO THE SEA.

At least that dispelled the rumors that she had landed on some abandoned island. One theory was that the Japanese were involved. When I asked the question the answer was:

NO.

Was she killed instantly?

YES.

When I asked what caused her to crash, he answered:

INTERFERENCE.

That answer made a lot of sense as all the individuals involved with her radio navigation system reported confusion and an inability to communicate with her. I inquired if there was something wrong with her instruments.

MAGNETIC FIELD FLUCTUATIONS.

Remembering what we had been told in a previous chapter about energy line intersections, my next question inquired if her plane instrumentation malfunctioned because she became involved with the fluctuations associated with ley line intersections. He replied:

YES.

We had also been told that earlier types of navigational devices were more likely to be influenced by the fluctuations related to the vortexes created by the ley lines. Apparently, the navigational devices on the plane flown by Amelia Earhart were no match for the natural disturbances.

JIMMY HOFFA, HIS DEMISE AND FINAL RESTING PLACE

No book on historical mysteries or conspiracies can be considered complete without attempting to determine the whereabouts of the body of the famous Teamster leader, Jimmy Hoffa. Hoffa was president of the International Brotherhood of Teamsters from 1958 until 1971. Well connected with organized crime, he was convicted of jury tampering, attempted bribery, and fraud. In 1967, he was imprisoned and sentenced to thirteen years. He continued serving as the Teamster leader while in prison. As part of a pardon agreement, he resigned his position in 1971 in return for a pardon from President Nixon. In 1975, he disappeared from outside a restaurant in Detroit and no trace of him or his remains have been found to this day. The flamboyant labor leader was officially declared dead in 1982. There are many theories as to where his body has been located for all these years.

I started by asking if Jimmy Hoffa was really dead. The answer came as a surprise.

HE KILLED HIMSELF.

When I asked why he would kill himself, the reply made a lot of sense when you consider his close friends.

TO SAVE HIS FAMILY.

So, you are saying that he committed suicide so his family would not be killed.

YES.

Was the mob behind the threats to kill his family?

YES.

Next, I asked the question that has been debated for the last forty years. Where is his body?

WATER.

Are you saying that he drowned himself?

YES.

Where did he drown himself?

HUDSON RIVER.

Apparently, he was taken to a location far from Detroit where there would be no search conducted for the body: New York. To borrow a line from *The Godfather*, "He sleeps with the fishes."

DISAPPEARANCE OF LOUIS LE PRINCE
THE TRUE INVENTOR OF MOTION PICTURES

Louis Le Prince is certainly not a household name but was actually the inventor of the first motion picture on paper film using a single lens camera. His work took place several years before Thomas Edison took credit for the discovery. La Prince mysteriously disappeared from a train in France in September 1890, just before he planned to visit America and patent his discovery. He was seen getting on the train but never got off it. His luggage and body were never located in spite of a huge search. Coincidentally, shortly after his disappearance, Edison attempted to take credit for the discovery. Since the time of his disappearance, there has been much conjecture that Edison was responsible for the disappearance, and probably the death, of Le Prince.

I am continually amazed at the depth of knowledge possessed by the spirit guides. When I asked what happened to Louis Le Prince, there was no hesitation:

THROWN OFF.

Someone had thrown the brilliant inventor off the train. My next question was why the body was never found.

RIVER.

That made a lot of sense. Whoever perpetrated the crime threw him off the train while it was on a bridge crossing a river. The real reason I included this segment was to find our if Thomas Edison was involved in the murder. His answer was:

NOT DIRECTLY.

Did Edison pay the killers?

NO.

Did he play any active role in the murder?

NONE.

According to our guide, the accusation that Thomas Edison had Louis Le Prince killed was false, but he certainly benefitted from his death.

WHO KILLED JONBENET RAMSEY?

The six-year-old body of JonBenet Ramsey was found in the Boulder, Colorado, home of her parents on December 25, 1996. Her body was found under a blanket, tied up with duct tape over her mouth. She had been killed by suffocation and a blow to the head. Her parents were initially suspected of killing the child, and the case made national headlines. JonBenet had participated in beauty pageants as a child, and her killer was never found. I started by asking if her parents had participated in the death of JonBenet. The guide was quick to answer:

No.

There had been a lot of guesswork in the papers that her brother was involved. Also reported at the time was the sighting of a strange man in the area. When I asked who killed the child, the answer was:

Neighbor.

To this day, the crime is unsolved. Hopefully some day they will be able to link the right person to the murder.

WHAT HAPPENED TO MADELINE MCCANN?

The case of the disappearance of four-year-old Madeline McCann gained worldwide notoriety when she disappeared from her bed in the Algarve region of Portugal in May 2007. Her parents had left the children alone to have dinner in a nearby restaurant. The local police misinterpreted DNA evidence and erroneously found that the child had died in the apartment instead of as part of an abduction. Her parents were suspected of killing her but were subsequently cleared of suspicion. No trace of the child has been found to this day. When I inquired as to what really happened to the missing child, the guide answered:

Kidnapped.

When I asked if she was still alive the reply was:

Yes.

Where is she now?

Australia.

Will he parents ever be reunited with her?

Unknown.

In this particular instance, the guide could not look into the future to see if the McCann family would ever see their daughter again. I believe there is still hope for the future.

WAS PRINCESS DIANA MURDERED?

One of the most loved individuals in the late 1900s was Great Britain's Princess Diana. Her wedding to the Prince of Wales took place on July 29, 1981. To the surprise of not many, their divorce became final on August 28, 1996, after she gave birth to two sons, heirs to the British throne. Shortly after the finalization of the divorce, it was announced that she was to become engaged to Dodi Fayed, a Muslim billionaire. On August 31, 1997, she suffered fatal injuries, along with Fayed, in an automobile accident in a tunnel near Paris. Many of the circumstances around her death seemed a bit suspicious.

I thought I would get right to the point and ask our guide if the Princess was murdered.

YES.

My guess is we all expected that answer. When I inquired who was behind the murder, the answer is also probably no surprise.

ROYAL FAMILY.

Who in the Royal family knew of the conspiracy to kill the Princess?

TWO KNEW.

Was one of them the Queen?

YES.

Did Charles know?

YES.

At the time of the accident there was a big deal made about it being caused by the paparazzi chasing the car of Diana and Fayed. Then articles appeared that the accident was caused by their driver having too much to drink. It seems like a lot of professional planning went into the incident. My next question asked if the whole thing was carried out by the English Secret Service.

INITIATED BY THEM.

It would be wise for the perpetrators of these conspiracies to realize that there are always witnesses to the crimes; they are just not of this dimension and are usually quite anxious for the truth to be known.

WHAT WAS BEHIND THE SANDY HOOK MASSACRE?

On December 14, 2012, we were all shocked by a mass shooting at the Sandy Hook Elementary School in Newtown, Connecticut. According to official reports, a twenty-year-old named Adam Lanza fatally shot twenty young children and six adult staff members of the school. When first responders arrived, Lanza committed suicide, preventing anyone from ever knowing what was really behind the shooting. Before driving to the school, Lanza apparently shot and killed his mother in her home. Almost as if prearranged, massive out-cries for gun control legislation flooded the air ways.

One evening I asked the guide if the Sandy Hook massacre was a government conspiracy. His reply could not have been any worse.

SADLY, YES.

Not wanting to believe what I just heard, I restated the question. Are you saying it was planned by our government?

PART OF THE NEW WORLD GUN CONTROL CAMPAIGN.

Some conspiracy theorists believe Adam Lanza was killed on the day before the massacre and was not really the shooter. I asked if Adam was killed the day before Sandy Hook.

THERE WERE TWO.

Two perpetrators?

YES, MOTHER KILLED PRIOR.

Was it a setup?

FATHER INVOLVED IN GOVERNMENT PROGRAMS.

Was the dad paid to set up son and mother?

SILENCING.

What was the attempt to show?

GOVERNMENT CONTROL.

Are you talking about Government control using fear and gun control?

YES, IT WILL BACKFIRE.

Will senators and congressmen ever reveal the plot?

YES.

At least there is hope that this horrific plot will be exposed sometime in the future. Once again I hope the information is wrong, but it was given to us by two separate guides. On another evening we were discussing the Boston Marathon bombings. The guide gave us an unexpected answer:

KNOWN TO CERTAIN OFFICIALS, SAME AS SANDY HOOK.

It should be becoming abundantly clear that our 2nd Amendment that gives the right to bear arms in our country is a huge deterrent to the New World Order people gaining power. The next time there is a mass shooting and politicians are on the news talking about gun control before the smell of gun powder is even out of the air, think about this segment of the book. ∞

CONCLUSION

Throughout the ages the free will of mankind has led to many instances of acts of conspiracy to harm and gain control over others. Our gift of spirit communication has allowed us in many instances to reach the actual souls of the victims of these acts. The more I worked on this book, the more aware I became that the victims wanted justice as they told the real facts that took place, not the so-called facts related by the perpetrators and oftentimes governments.

I hope this book brings justice to the souls involved and better understanding of what really takes place to affect the living. It should also be obvious that there are no secrets to those on the other side, and the guides and spirits are quite anxious to tell the truth. All they need is a channel to pierce the veil that separates the living and those who have passed.

BIBLIOGRAPHY

Begich, Nick and Jeane Manning. *Angels Don't Play This HAARP: Advances in Tesla Technology*. Alaska: Earthpulse Press, 1995.

Bord, J. and Colin Bord. *The Bigfoot Casebook*. Harrisburg, PA: Stackpole Books, 1982.

Bord, Janet, Colin Bord, and Loren Coleman. *Bigfoot Casebook Updated: Sightings and Encounters from 1818 to 2004*. Michigan: Pine Woods Press, 2005.

Childress, David Hatcher. *Anti-Gravity & the World Grid*.Illinois: Adventures Unlimited Press, 2013.

Ehanamani, Dr. A. Ross. *Crazy Horse, The Real Reason for the Battle of the Little Big Horn*. Colorado: Wiconi Waste, 2000.

Greenwell, J. R. *Florida Giant Penguin Hoax Revealed*. ISC Newsletter, 7(4), Winter. 1988.

Miller, David. *Custer's Fall: The Native American Side of the Story*. New York: Plume Publishing, 1992.

Powers, Thomas. *How Little Bighorn Was Won. Smithsonian Magazine*, November, 2010.

Stein, G. *Bigfoot, Encyclopedia of the Paranormal*, Buffalo: Prometheus, 1996.

Stone, Roger. *The Man Who Killed Kennedy: The Case Against LBJ*. New York: Skyhorse Publishing, 2014.

Strohm, Barry. *Afterlife, What Really Happens on the Other Side*. Atglen, PA: Schiffer Publishing, 2015.

Vankin, Jonathan and John Whalen. *The World's Greatest Conspiracies*. New York: Kensington Publishing, 2010.

Wilcox, Robert. *Target Patton: The Plot to Kill General George S. Patton*. Washington, DC: Regency History Publishing, 2014.

Websites

www.aboutbillythekid.com/index.html

http://ancientexplorers.com/blog/ley-lines/

http://blog.nationalmediamuseum.org.uk/2013/08/29/louis-le-prince-created-the-first-ever-moving-pictures/

http://findmadeleine.com/home.html

http://law.rightpundits.com/?p=3315

http://theappendix.net/issues/2014/1/bandit-resurrections-who-was-the-real-sundance-kid

http://utah.com/old-west/butch-cassidy

https://usahitman.com/tuhoh/#prettyPhoto/0/

www.angelfire.com/mi2/billythekid/brushy.html

www.bibliotecapleyades.net/mapas_ocultotierra/esp_mapa_ocultotierra_12.htm

www.biography.com/people/jimmy-hoffa-9341063

www.biography.com/people/jonbenet-ramsey-12986606

www.colinandrews.net/JuliaSetStory.html

www.cracked.com/article_19765_the-5-creepiest-disappearances-that-nobody-can-explain.html

www.csicop.org/si/show/bigfoot_at_50_evaluating_a_half-century_of_bigfoot_evidence

www.etcgroup.org/issues/climate-geoengineering

www.gonomad.com/21-features/990-following-the-trail-of-butch-cassidy-and-the-sundance-kid-in-bolivia#ibQ5KWAr4iyqbUQ8.99

www.heroesatmargraten.com/the-death-of-general-george-s-patton.html

www.history.com/news/history-lists/6-things-you-might-not-know-about-butch-cassidy

www.huffingtonpost.com/bill-chameides/obama-takes-bold-step-to_b_5069973.html

www.ibiblio.org/hyperwar/OnlineLibrary/photos/usnshtp/ac/w1ac-2.htm cyclops

www.joshuastevens.net/visualization/squatch-watch-92-years-of-bigfoot-sightings-in-us-and-canada/

www.myforrestgumplife.com/who_killed_jfk.html

www.pattonhq.com/textfiles/resign.html

www.rense.com/general76/hunt.htm

www.rollingstone.com/culture/features/the-last-confession-of-e-howard-hunt-20070405?page=4

www.smithsonianmag.com/ist/?next=/history/abandoned-ship-the-mary-celeste-174488104/

www.subterraneanbases.com/virginia-s-underground/

www.vortexmaps.com/hagens-grid-google.php